Pain and Suffering

Friend or Foe?

Other books by this author deal with heritage, family, faith, and other inspiring and life-affecting topics:

My Mother Built the Fire
The Fire Still Burns
The Cadillac Years
Somewhere Beyond Yesterday
Beyond Today
After Tomorrow

Pain and Suffering
Friend or Foe?

Jack Hilliard

O'MORE
PUBLISHING
FRANKLIN, TENNESSEE

Pain and Suffering: Friend or Foe

ISBN-10 0-9800285-0-7
ISBN-13 978-0-9800285-0-8

Edited by Jessa Rose Sexton
Cover design by Paula Rozelle Bagnall
Book Block design by Paula Rozelle Bagnall
Illustrations by Jennifer Savage

Published by:
O'More Publishing
A Division of O'More College of Design
423 South Margin St.
Franklin, TN 37064 U.S.A

Dedication

This book is affectionately dedicated to one of the most noble, encouraging, heroic men I have ever been blessed to know. There is absolutely no way to measure the accomplishments and good works of this beloved friend and brother-in-Christ! He has touched more lives and blessed more people than one could count. Heaven will surely be filled with faithful servants like this man. There are many reasons I want to go to heaven, but the thought of a place filled with such people persuades me to take every step I can in that direction.

This book is dedicated to Mr. Bob Faulk.

A chapter in the back of this book will further explain the reason for this dedication.

Contents

Acknowledgements

I am grateful to so many who have read my other books and encouraged me to continue writing.

Two congregations where I have presented a series of lessons on the subject material of this book have been very persuasive: the Sitka Church of Christ in Milan, Tennessee, and the Church at Gulf Shores, Alabama. Others have also made requests to see this information in writing.

I appreciate my dear wife who has endured many hours of my attention to this endeavor. Also, my son, Mark Hilliard, and granddaughter, Jessa Hilliard Sexton, who have encouraged my writing this and other books and have assisted me in preparing this for publication.

I am grateful to O'More Publishing for taking on this project and to Jessa who is my capable typist and editor.

Preface

Pain and Suffering: Friend or Foe belongs in every library, though not just on the shelf; it can benefit anyone who reads and digests it. The happiest or most miserable can derive encouragement from this tried and true information. Taking at least three years in preparation, the book is based on a lifetime of study, personal experiences, and relationships: relationships with some of the most highly educated, with those lacking formal education, with some of the wealthiest, and with some of the poorest people all over the United States and in some foreign countries. Much study and years of observing people in all walks of life have molded the ideas projected in this volume.

The book presents a common sense and scriptural approach to acceptance of pain and suffering as well as an application of resources including both pleasant and unpleasant examples.

Those who have encouraged me and molded my life, who helped me grow up, counsel, teach, and write, have also been further inspiration for this book: my parents, wife, children, in-laws, teachers at Freed-Hardeman University, and fellow classmates from first grade to the pursuit of higher education.

Further encouragement and inspiration has been derived from those who have learned, applied themselves, and taken the time to write books of a common interest to this one.

Dr. Kippy Myers, Professor of Freed-Hardeman University and author of *The Problem of Suffering*

Dr. Bill Flatt, a Christian counselor and author of *Restoring My Soul*

Bob Spurling, *Don't Ever Give Up*

Dr. Mark Hilliard, President of O'More College of Design and author of *Spirit-Ritual* and *Catcher of Dreams*

Frank Chessor, minister and author of *Portrait of God*

Willard Tate, *Habits of a Loving Heart*

These have prompted my mind and stirred me, bringing up memories of past experiences and lessons that I have applied to fifty-seven years of experience as a Gospel minister, missionary, counselor, and author.

All Bible quotations are from the King James Version unless otherwise noted.

Pain and Suffering: Friend or Foe?

In many cases, whether or not pain is a friend or foe depends on one's outlook on life. We can think of it as a privilege or drudgery. It may be the difference in an optimist or a pessimist. We look at everything that happens from some point of view. If we conclude all is bad, then no matter what happens we will see every experience in a bad connotation. If life is seen as a privilege, then this optimistic view can put a good spin on even our problems, disappointments, and suffering. If optimistic vision allows us to think of the future and others, we may be able to see past our brief pain to the possible good result. The future will be brighter, and the load will be lighter. Necessary painful surgery or bitter medicine may be unpleasant at the time, but is often the only means to health and well being in the future.

Much depends on the confidence we have in the physician, as in the previous example, or in the Great

Physician, as in our everyday lives. Belief or disbelief in tomorrow—hope or lack of it—can make all the difference in how pain is felt: hope can reduce pain or bring healing later. Do we concentrate on present pain and multiply it, or do we see in it a good result, often reducing even today's misery?

Are our goals big enough and high enough to be worth the effort to attain them? Every good thing has a cost! If the cost hurts more than the expected outcome, we are doomed to the status quo. Failure always results in misery! Misery can only be reduced and cured by reaching and climbing above it. When we do, we will be stronger—better—and enjoy a great feeling of attainment.

Misery can only be cured by climbing above it.

I recently noted a quote from an unknown source. It is a good idea for a good life: "For every evil under the sun, there is a remedy or there is none. If there is one, seek till you find it. If there is none, never mind it." The inspired wisdom of Solomon provides this helpful information: "To everything there is a season, and a time to every purpose under the heaven" (Ecclesiastes 3:1). He proceeds to enlarge on this principle throughout that chapter.

Through this book, I hope to expound on the title, give you clarity of the phrase "Friend or Foe," and offer you encouragement and help. If successful in these goals, all efforts and time will be richly rewarded!

Why Does the God We Believe in Cause Pain and Suffering?

The very first objective of this book is to convince the honest inquirer that God does not cause pain and suffering. We will begin by addressing some of the oldest views on the subject.

Judges 6:1-13 relates how the children of Israel had suffered at the hands of the Midianites. They cried out to God, blaming Him for their miserable state. An angel was sent, and he told Gideon, "God is with you." Gideon responded, "If God is with us, why all this pain and suffering?"

This same old attitude has been echoed through the ages. People still ask, why did God send cancer, fire, war, death?

The Epicureans referred to in Acts 12:18 promoted this view. If there is a God who desires to prevent suffering and cannot, then He is not powerful. If He has the power to prevent suffering and does not, then He is not good. If he has both desire and power, then why do we still experience pain and suffering? They then concluded, "There is no God."

Sadly enough many today, including some highly educated, still promote this sad view.

What we can conclude is God does not fit the mold of many people. For example, some of the most popular and wealthy television personalities have said, "Your God may condemn some practice but my god does not." The fact is our own self-made god could not even be as powerful and intelligent as we are and would be of no real, permanent value. The self-made gods mentioned in Acts 17 were shown by the inspired Paul to serve no real need. The result was another disappointment added to all the others.

The God who created us can cause even pain to produce a useful purpose!

It is obviously a well-known fact that both God and pain do exist. Thus the well-informed and honest mind is forced to recognize that the God who created us can cause even pain to produce a useful purpose!

God does not cause pain! How do we know this? For one thing, suffering is a type of temptation, and "God cannot be tempted with evil, neither tempteth He any man" (James 1:13). The next two verses conclude that every man is tempted when he is drawn away by his own lust and enticed. "Then when lust hath conceived, it bringeth forth sin," and "when sin is finished it bringeth forth death" (James 1:14-15). These words are not the conclusion of a mere man but words God inspired James to pen.

Some would blame all pain and suffering on God. Others would place all the suffering and problems on others. Still others blame all problems, pain, and suffering on themselves. None of these choices is a viable option. Much blame can fall on what we have done, and some may be attributed to others. The fact is no blame should be placed on God!

❖ ❖ ❖

There are two kinds of suffering. One type is natural causes or those caused by nature such as storms, floods, and earthquakes. The other type is moral causes or personal sins.

It is a Biblical teaching and proven fact that disregard for any law produces pain of some degree or type. This is experienced in the natural, physical realm and also in the moral or spiritual realm.

Some would argue that an all-powerful God could control the laws of nature. Consider the law of gravity (a wise part of God's creation). God could prevent me from being injured from falling from a building and hitting the ground by changing that law, but His overall wise plan knows the results to all other facts and people involved. If the law of gravity were to become ineffective, fruit would not fall from the tree. People and objects would just be floating around in space.

Fatal chaos would prevail if God's natural laws were hindered.

If God withheld rain on my field think of what could happen to my neighbor's parched soil. If my neighbor received a needed shower, how would the same rain affect my newly mown hay?

We bring problems on ourselves by building in areas unfit for the structure or the needs of human beings. We infringe on animal habitats then blame the animals for acting like they are designed to act. Men build on cliffs and blame God when their beautiful houses are destroyed by a natural mud slide. One contractor built houses in a rural area where the soil would not "perk." As a result, the sewage system could not be absorbed by that soil.

Disregard for any established law always produces pain!

Disregard for any established law always produces pain! An all-wise God who created us also wisely created laws designed for our well being. It is neither fair nor wise to blame God when we suffer because we disregard His laws.

Perhaps God allows some suffering to be produced from natural causes because He can see the end result. He can know that the strong and faithful can and will be made better rather than overcome by some unpleasant experiences. We will give further attention to this idea later on.

Why do men suffer? There are many causes: God is not responsible for any of them!

Let me consider my own suffering. When I suffer, it must mean the pain is bad enough for me to recognize its presence. Do I then blame God, who is always good and on whom I am dependent for everything? Or do I consider the other possibilities?

God is opposed to all sin, and sin—my own or someone else's—is the reason behind all suffering. (Remember, the first sin was the cause of the first suffering.) God's love and grace brought me into this world, and God loved me so much He allowed His own Son to suffer and die so I could go back to Him. Can I expect that same God would deliver me to pain and sorrow if I lived in a world where all observed His laws and will? We live in a sinful, fallen world, and, therefore, we live in a world with suffering and pain.

Remember God's Suffering for Us

It eases our pain when we remember our Lord suffered for us.

One man lost a son to death and lost his faith. His reasoning was, "Where was God when my son died?" His wise friend responded, "The same place He was when His Son died!" Don't ever forget God so loved us that He gave His only begotten Son so that our active faith in Him could redeem our sinful souls and make a heavenly home available to us where no sin or suffering is ever found!

We suffer because of the misuse of some of our greatest blessings. For example, one of our most special blessings is a result of the fact that God made us free moral agents, able to make our own decisions. Sometimes the decisions we make bring suffering to our lives.

Do we chain up or lock up our loved ones to protect them? Of course not, because we realize a degree of freedom is essential to their maturity. In example, a dear friend of ours had a four-year-old daughter who had a brain tumor. It cost the family intense suffering for their child to go through surgery. The terrible pain was relieved, but she was left blind. Throughout the ordeal, the family had several choices. Their first choice was to deny the surgery to prevent the possible blindness and leave her to endure torture of pain as long as she lived. The second choice was to blame God for the tumor or blindness or both. Their precious faith would not permit that. The third choice was to overprotect the daughter and make her impairment far worse. They chose, rather, to watch her carefully but allow her freedom to take some risks and learn to be wonderfully independent. She later attended a special school to learn how to develop skills that gave her more independence. Out of her loss, this girl became a blessing and encouragement to our family and to all who were blessed to know her.

We are free because God loves us. As a result, we are free to make choices. Our Creator has also informed us that every choice has a consequence. Wrong choices produce bad consequences. That is balanced by the beautiful fact that good choices bring good, rewarding consequences.

A close friend of mine lost a dear son in a horrible auto accident. The father did not blame God; he knew drugs were involved, and he said, "He made some bad choices." As terrible as the loss was, it would have been multiplied had the father chosen to blame God, the greatest source of comfort.

The first couple on this earth was given only one limiting law. They were not to eat of the tree of knowledge of good and evil in the beautiful garden. Adam and Eve chose to disregard God's law and be deceived by their only enemy. We all know the result of that bad choice recorded in Genesis 3. Also, we all still suffer the consequence of that horrible decision. It was not God's fault nor our fault, but we suffer today for this wrong choice as well as the wrong choices of others.

Joshua 5:39-40 records a marvelous choice we all enjoy today: "Choose you this day whom you will serve." To choose God always brings blessings. To choose not to accept God and His will always brings dreadful consequences.

John 5:39-40 requires that we search the scripture to be informed about God and His ways. This inspired writer reminds the reader that a decision must be made, explaining the correct decision and the result of making the wrong decision—not receiving life.

Judges 6:1 tells us that the children of Israel did evil, and the Lord delivered them into the hands of their enemies for seven years. It seems the Israelites later forget that their loss was the result of their own evil choice when they wonder why God had allowed their sad plight. Modern people are prone to forget God's warnings and wonder why we suffer and blame God, just as the Israelites did. God has been fair to inform mankind of every age that our decisions are directly linked to our consequences. Shall we learn from the effects of others' decisions as well as our own sins, or shall we choose to stumble along in the darkness of bad information and the temptation of our bitter enemy?

A worthy New Testament example of God's light is recorded in Romans 6:16-18. It is up to us to choose who will be our master—sin or righteousness. In Romans, those who chose to quit serving sin and obeyed from their heart the doctrine of God were freed from sin and became the servants of righteousness. Verse 23 clearly reminds us that "the wages of sin is death; but the gift of God is eternal life through Jesus Christ our Lord." That there is a decision to be made is clear, and the results of the decision are equally clear.

It is up to us to choose who will be our master—sin or righteousness.

Our Own Sins May Be the Reason for Our Suffering

Let it be said again that our own personal sins are not the only reason for our pain; however, it may be good to conduct a personal examination first when we seek the cause of unpleasant situations in our lives. This personal responsibility is called to our attention in Ezekiel 18:4, 20 which makes a plain statement about cause and effect: the soul that sins shall die.

The first New Testament case of discipline in the Lord's church is recorded in Acts 5:1-11. The basic love for personal attention and material gain coupled together to persuade Ananias and Sapphira to allow Satan to tempt them to sin and then lie to the Holy Spirit, adding sin to sin. The consequence was physical and spiritual death.

Saul of Tarsus was one of the best educated men of his age. He always acted with the approval of his conscience. He was extremely religious. In fact, he belonged to the strictest sect of religion, the Pharisees. Despite all his advantages, his personal prejudice against the Lord and His people forced him to do things that he thought were right at the time. We can see quickly that what he thought was right, though, actually made him a persecutor of the Lord and His church and created much horror for Christianity (Acts 9:26).

When struck blind on the road to Damascus, Saul was personally confronted by the Lord and suffered for his misconduct and heinous sins. Asking the Lord for a way out of his terrible dilemma, Saul was presented with a choice to turn his life around. He gladly responded to the Gospel and became a great servant of Christ. Before this conversion, many great people suffered because of his actions. However, when he became obedient to the Lord, his actions immediately and always afterwards became a blessing to untold amounts of people. His story is an example of a man's sins causing the suffering of others, but it is also one of a man's sins (even sins he did not realize he was committing at the time) bringing about his own suffering. In the end, though, good choices brought personal blessings and blessings to others.

God warns His people in Joshua 24:20, "If you forsake the Lord, He will do you hurt and consume you after He has done you good." This is a fair warning that consistent faithfulness to God is essential to enjoy His promises. When we sin, we suffer the consequences of our actions.

Every man shall die for his own sins in the warning recorded in II Chronicles 25:4. The bright side of this verse is simply that, though we might suffer some pain for the sins of others, we do not have to bear the guilt of those sins. We still suffer the consequences of Adam's sins, but not the guilt.

It is also necessary we recognize that when our sins are forgiven, by the grace of God through our obedient faith, we may still bear the scars of those sins. We suffer pain and anguish when we offend our conscience. There is no escape! Those who claim a loving God will not punish anyone should recognize that the loving Creator placed within each one of us this strong instrument of punishment. His loving care put it there to help protect us from more serious pain.

Problems do not have to be enemies.

It is imperative that we realize that suffering may result in a better life; problems do not have to be enemies.

There are many examples of this fact in my personal life. All three of our children experienced a bitter disappointment in former jobs, jobs that had been excellent at one time. Our oldest son was deeply hurt when a job he enjoyed became no longer suitable for him. As a result, he decided to further his education. After earning his doctor's degree and moving to a better job, he was presented with the opportunity to return to Freed-Hardeman University to teach psychology and counseling. He also had an opportunity to work with some other Christian counselors in a private practice. In 2006, he was made Director of Children Services in West Tennessee.

Our second son had earned several promotions in a health organization. He loved his work and was very successful. When the organization began a new system for fund raising he could not accept, he suffered much anguish. He too decided to further his education. As a result of superior performance, he was offered a job at the university he attended. He taught classes at Middle Tennessee State University. Also, the very summer he defended his doctoral dissertation, he was given a job as the academic dean of O'More College of Design in Franklin, Tennessee. A year and a half later, he was made president. Throughout his work at the college, he has accomplished many great goals, received honors, and made other great achievements.

Our daughter had achieved great success at a very reputable insurance company. After many achievements for that organization, some disappointing changes in the system forced her to leave this job that she had enjoyed so much. She also chose to earn another degree. While teaching at a business college, she was presented with an opportunity to teach for the University of Tennessee and was soon made director of their Selmer campus. This has proved to be a very useful and fulfilling experience for her.

The great success stories of each of our precious children could never have been possible without the extremely painful chapters. My wife and I often talk about how every disappointment and painful experience of our lives have resulted in something very good we are so grateful for.

Sometimes it is because of our own sins that we suffer, and sometimes suffering comes unexpectedly, in the middle of a joyful time of our lives. In any case, our reaction to pain in our lives will make all the difference.

The author and his wife
with their three children in the early 1970s.

We May Suffer Because of the Sins of Others

Perhaps as many or more suffer because of the sins or actions of others than from our own sins. Many who suffer for others' mistakes are good people and completely innocent victims.

For example, I know of a faithful Gospel preacher and true servant of God who was killed by a drunk driver. In another scenario, three teen-age boys were killed by drunk drivers; they lost their lives and never had an opportunity to develop into useful, prosperous adults. Not only did these people suffer and die because of someone else's sins, but their family members and loved ones suffered loss as well. Most who read this are also aware of pain and death caused by someone choosing to disregard God's laws.

Even mistakes can bring about misery. Innocent children and adults sometimes suffer because of the errors of doctors. One of the most precious, inspiring students who ever attended Freed-Hardeman was born without arms. A doctor had prescribed a drug for her mother that produced this result. Mother, daughter, and doctor were innocent in the matter, but the outcome was still painful for all. Overcoming her disadvantages, the young lady learned to live a fairly normal life, had a useful practice in social work, and raised two children. Despite her physical limitations, she became a hard-working and encouraging person. She said most handicaps were in people's minds. It is possible she would never have accomplished some of the good she did had she been born physically normal or possessed a different attitude.

Ignorance is a major factor in the suffering of many good people. For example, Asbestos, D.D.T., and Agent Orange were all designed and used to help people, but the outcome was very detrimental. Many suffer diabetes with all its hindrances. It may be caused by a lack of information from a doctor or the individual or by bad eating habits.

When we are discouraged to the point of despair, remember what our Lord went through for us.

The Christian martyr Stephen lost his good life because of the ignorant prejudice and hatred of others in Acts 7. This still happens in many places today. As this book is being written, similar actions are happening to countless people in the Middle East.

Few people have suffered like Paul, and much of his pain was inflicted by others. It is written in II Corinthians 11:23-33 that Jesus Christ, the only perfect person who ever walked this earth, suffered beyond our comprehension. It is interesting to note that even though prejudiced, ignorant people (people who did not believe He was Christ) inflicted such horrible pain, Christ allowed it to occur to prevent our eternal suffering in hell. When we are discouraged to the degree of unbearable despair, we will do well to remember what our Lord went through for us. He certainly understands our pain, especially our pain brought on by the actions of others. God made Him who knew no sin to be sin for us, that we might be made the righteousness of God in Him (II Corinthians 5:21).

Some Causes for Suffering

We suffer because we were born into a world of sin! There may be several reasons why a person drowns; however, the first reason is because he or she was in the water in the first place. Because of our surroundings, we all sin and come short of the glory of God (Romans 3:23). We daily suffer the consequences of sin in various degrees. The final result is "the wages of sin is death" (Romans 6:23). However, the gift of God is eternal life through Christ Jesus our Lord. Sometimes suffering may be the motive for changing a lifestyle and ultimately accepting what God sent His Son to die for: Christ died for us all (John 3:16). It follows that all who accept His gift through obedient faith can reap the benefits.

It is foolish to blame God for the condition of the world because He did not create the kind of world we dwell in. His creation was good and perfect in every way. Man disobeyed God, rejected His perfect world, and introduced the sin that spoiled God's perfect creation. (We will deal more fully with this later on.)

Our faith is our strongest ally. I John 5:4 reminds us that faith is the victory that overcomes the world. The choice is ours, and Christ is obviously the best choice; the sooner we realize this and make the right choices, the quicker we unload the burden of sin and its accompanying pain. In this respect, pain can be a friend instead of a foe—a learning tool or an avenue to blessings.

Faith will not cause us to believe we will not suffer pain, but faith lets us believe in God when He promises we will not suffer above our ability to bear it; we will not suffer alone, without God on our side. Our Lord, who knew no sin, suffered for our sin. He understands us and can and will help us if we accept His help (I Corinthians 10:13).

Our enemy is Satan! He is the enemy of God and all good. Do we believe he is stronger than God? As surely as we believe that God is stronger, it makes sense to accept Him and His remedy for sin. The theme of the great book of Revelation is that Christ will win!

> We accept His help by a responsive faith.

The love, grace, and mercy of God provides the cleansing blood and saving Gospel to redeem us from the results of sin and to enjoy God's help in this life. We accept His help by a responsive faith.

We have no control over when and where we were born. We do have a choice about getting in dangerous water, as seen in the illustration at the beginning of this chapter, or where we go and what we do in this world. God's people are in the world but not of the world (John 17:14).

John made the fact clear in John 16:33 that "in the world ye shall have tribulations." We should not be like Demas, who in II Timothy 4:10 chose the way of the world over working for the Lord. God does give us a choice and provides a number of reasons for choosing His way. Surely one of the reasons we consider in view of the subject of this book is to relieve ourselves of much pain and suffering by God's comfort now and all pain and suffering by God's grace in the hereafter.

False, Unreal Expectations of God

Many of us will remember the song "I Didn't Promise You a Rose Garden." God did not promise the future world a garden like Eden after Adam and Eve allowed sin to spoil it. Nor could God promise, in our best interest, some things we would like. In His wisdom, God knows His standards cannot always agree with ours; this would bring Him down to our human, not all-knowing level. What would such a God be like? Could He meet our real needs? The results of such a God would often have a negative effect. The self-made gods of some in the past were like men. They were subject to the passions of weak mankind. In Old Testament days and in the days of Paul the people offered sacrifices, even sacrificing the lives of people, but not out of love. These sacrifices were designed to appease the wrath of their false gods. In my visit to the Bible Lands, I saw ruins of material temples made by deceived men in order to worship their unreal gods. Our God does not dwell in temporary, material, man-made structures. Our God made us—we did not make Him—and our God knows better than we do (Acts 17: 24-25).

The gods of man's making could not make or fulfill any promises. Our God makes no promises that are not in our best interest. He did not promise we would never suffer pain or disappointment; if I labored under the false impression that He made such a promise, then I would be hurt and disappointed every time I felt pain. Our God of honesty, integrity, and fairness tells us clearly, "All who will live godly in Christ Jesus shall suffer persecution" (II Timothy 3:12). Could we love and trust any other kind of god?

Our God makes no promises that are not in our best interest.

Think of the doctor or dentist who tells you that some procedure will produce no pain. Then, when you experience it, you do feel the pain. Could you ever trust that person again? Remember I Corinthians 10:13 which says, "Temptation is common to man, but a God of love provides strength and help." He also promises eternal salvation to those who faithfully serve Him to the end. Revelation chapter 3 and 4 promise special blessings to all who overcome.

It affords great comfort to accept the assurance that God never sends temptation, never allows it to befall on us, without providing a way of escape. We choose whether or not we accept His grace and apply His plan.

Short-Term Pain Often Produces Long-Time Gain

Work or exercise may produce much pain, but the end results may provide many benefits: better health, weight control, more strength, and improved appearance, to name a few. Many of us who grew up with hard physical labor were much better prepared to overcome problems with body or organs, to recover from serious surgery, etc. I am fully persuaded that I would not be alive today if my body had not been prepared by hard work in my youth.

The old adage "no pain, no gain" is true for the most part. The same senses are often affected and used to produce both joy and suffering. If we totally eradicate one—joy or suffering—we hinder both.

Pangs of hunger improve taste for food. I have always had a healthy appetite and really enjoyed most foods. Some were a very great pleasure for me. After open heart surgery, I endured a three month experience of little appetite and pleasure in any food. My good wife would ask, "What do you want me to prepare for you today?" My response was, "It makes no difference; it all tastes just alike, and it all tastes like cardboard." What a very special reward it was to reach a point where I enjoyed food again!

God also blessed me with greater appreciation and taste for more healthy foods in recent years. This was developed some years ago when I learned that some of my favorite foods were creating serious health problems that would have resulted in death. I was amazed at how quickly I adjusted to my change in diet and learned to fully enjoy more health-conscious foods.

When I was a young boy, my mother and I picked cotton every fall for me to buy school clothes. Much of the time we picked for the Jenkins and Pike families. We took a sack lunch to the field, and whatever limited food we had sure tasted delicious after a hard morning's work. Then, at noon, Mrs. Edith Jenkins would invite us to their table and prepare us a tall glass of iced tea. I don't think I had ever before, or have ever since, tasted such refreshing, delicious tea. I think I could make a long speech about "All I ever needed to know I learned in the cotton patch." I well remember how great it was to fall in bed, tired to the bone, and to wake totally refreshed from a good night's sleep. Our hard work in the field made the reward of the tea that much sweeter and the night's rest that much more appreciated.

Wise Solomon would have agreed with me. In Ecclesiastes 5:12 he writes, "The sleep of a laboring man is sweet; whether he eat little or much; but the abundance of the rich will not suffer him to sleep." In verse 18 he adds, "Behold that which I have seen; it is good and comely for me to eat and drink and enjoy the good of his labor that he taketh under the sun all the days of his life, which God giveth him; for it is his portion."

The wealthy may enjoy some things that the poor will never possess, but there are so many things that money cannot secure that the poor fully appreciate.

I recall being ill as a young boy over a period of time; when I recovered, I felt like I could outrun a deer. Life took on a whole new perspective.

Pain makes heaven more desirable. Paul aptly describes this attitude in Philippians 3:7-11 and concludes that all gain was loss when compared to the proper relationship to Christ. He writes that what was once so valuable to him, when lost, made him realize that it was but waste material compared to the knowledge of Christ. He even references fellowship in Christ's suffering a blessing when one can comprehend the gain of resurrection with Christ.

Pain makes heaven more desirable.

It is a great fact—the appeal of the world could keep us from heaven if we did not recognize how bad pain is and how great it will be to experience a state where absolutely no pain exists.

Now suppose all good ended when this failing world became ashes? To what end were our experiences here? Only evil, pain, and temporary things are here, but there is no end to the bliss and joy of a heavenly home.

In the light of such facts, is pain a foe or a friend?

Other Reasons for Pain and Suffering

Earlier we alluded to the question often posed: why did God make the world as He did? Just now we want to spend some more time together considering this question and some reasonable answers.

The first answer is an emphatic "He didn't!"

Remember we stressed earlier that God pronounced His total creation "good and very good." What happened? Man spoiled God's perfect creation. There are many ways this has been accomplished. People poison our environment. We throw out garbage and change our landscape; we refuse to leave dangerous areas and construct dwellings in areas that place us in jeopardy. Natural order is disrupted to appease our hungry appetites. Invading the habitat of wild animals, we force them into ours. Some use fertilizer to build destructive bombs. We insist on diets that poison our bodies, ingest abusive amounts of sugar, starch, etc, and overuse the substitutes for sugar and other foods. Some insist on the use of alcohol, tobacco, and other drugs known to be harmful to our bodies; others abuse even good drugs and foods to their detriment. Desiring the short term pleasure without regard to the long term negative results, we ignore God's warnings of some of these things.

Lust demands satisfaction, bringing social diseases and poisons upon us. Some insist on lifestyles that are specifically forbidden by the Eternal Creator who alone knows what is best for us. It is easy to forget or reject the great, powerful truths that our bodies are the temple of God; we have been bought and paid for with a great price. Therefore, our bodies are to be protected and cared for and used to glorify God (I Corinthians 6:19-20). Are we so unlearned or consumed by our own desires that we are unable to recognize the difference this physical devotion to God would make in our own personal lives, our happiness, and the entire world? In I Corinthians 9, the inspired Paul affirms that those who reject God's standard and abuse the body cannot inherit the Kingdom of God. Only when we accept that God's kingdom is far superior to the kingdom of the world will we help restore the world to a better, happier state and quit blaming God for the sad state of our earthly dwelling; then we can accept God's gracious offer of a perfect state when this world ends.

Social diseases are responsible for much of the agonizing pain we see all about us today. Lifestyle is responsible for 90% of AIDS cases today: sexual choices and drug use. We have already noted that I Corinthians 6:9-10 condemns sexual immorality; sexual sins are also condemned in Leviticus 18:20-24. Again God's advice—His commands—if kept, would prevent and eliminate many of the most disturbing problems and pains of today.

Another example is that most of us suffer continuous tax increases and higher insurances costs. One of the major reasons for this is the abuse and sins of others, possibly greed or selfishness.

Much of our suffering is due to humanity, not divinity.

Can we blame our doctors when we reject their prescriptions and fail to experience healing? Isn't it even more irresponsible to blame our Father and Creator for our status produced by our refusal to accept His wise instruction? The fact is so much of our suffering is due to humanity, not divinity.

Are You Satisfied with the World?

Most of us who would consider the question, "Are you satisfied with the world," would answer with a hasty, "NO!" How does our life reflect our answer?

If the world in which you live is a disagreeable place, try changing yourself. It will be surprising how quickly we'll get results and how much the world around us will improve. If people are unfriendly, is it because of what they see in us? Try putting on a smile for those who are stormy; speak a word of thankfulness in those conversations that are filled with complaints. Try laughing a bit to benefit those who are down-hearted. When we change our approach to the world, the world will change. As surely as we look for evil in others, we'll find it; just as certainly, if we look for good, we'll find it.

We can improve the world by helping people, and we can best help people by self-improvement. An application of the golden rule will improve self, people in general, and the world as a whole. "Therefore all things whatsoever ye would that men should do to you ye do even so to them" (Matthew 7:12).

You may have heard the question, "Are you part of the problem or a part of the solution?" We can never improve a bad situation by becoming a part of it. Even an ant can go along with the crowd. When we join the negative group, we hinder self and others. In our world of discontent, fighting, division, selfishness, demonstration, and destruction we can change the course of history and improve the world or go along with it to ruin. Paul told Christian people to not be conformed to the world but to be transformed (Romans 12:1-2).

> We can never improve a bad situation by becoming a part of it.

If we are not satisfied with the world, let us be different from the world, improve ourselves, and watch the world change.

This World

Author Unknown

This world is not so bad a world
As some would like to make it
Though whether good or whether bad,
Depends on how we make it.
For if we scold and fret all day
From dewy morn till even,

This world will ne'er afford to man
A foretaste here of heaven.

❖

This world in truth's as good a world
As e'er was known to any
Who have not seen another world,
And these are very many;
And if the men and women, too,
Have plenty of employment,
Those surely must be hard to please
Who cannot find employment.

❖

The world is quite a clever world
In rain or pleasant weather,
If people would but learn to live
In harmony together;
Nor seek to burst the kindly bond
By love and peace cemented,
And learn the best of lessons, yet
To always be contented.

❖ ❖ ❖

Attitudes in Life Change like the Stroke of a Brush

My wife and I share the hobby of oil painting, and though we do not profess to be artists, we have learned many principles that apply not only to painting but also to life.

In some of our first efforts we were working on water scenes, and the water kept giving the appearance of flowing uphill. We called our teacher, Woody Douglass, and asked her what the problem was. She recognized immediately that we were turning our brush strokes the wrong way and explained how the stroke of the brush created the appearance of water flowing up or downstream or standing still. The lesson we learned also determined whether we had a mountain or a valley.

If we allow our attitude in life to be represented by the brush, we can make a vital application: what life appears to be is determined far more from what is within than from outside influence. When we learned how to use our brush strokes properly, we could create the proper landscape.

There is a wonderful little booklet called "A Better World Begins with Me." That statement is so true.

It's not so much what happens to us as what happens in us that makes life good or bad. If the world were all mountains or valleys or level land, it would not be nearly so beautiful. Life doesn't always have to be an uphill climb; it has its highs and lows, and how we view these times has everything to do with our success in life.

It's not so much what happens to us as what happens in us that makes life good or bad.

The artist must turn the brush different ways, the strokes must change to capture a scene of beauty, and the Master Artist has turned the stroke of the brush to give us a beautiful world of changes rather than a dull "look the same" world.

As we each paint our own world, we must remember that we are the ones who change the stroke of the brush. "For as he thinketh in his heart so is he" (Proverbs 23:7). Paul advises that we think on things that are true, honest, just, pure, lovely, excellent, and praiseworthy in Philippians 4:8. Also, in Philippians 3:13-15, Paul recommends that we follow his example of forgetting anything that hinders us, setting high goals, and reaching for them. He continues his advice in Philippians 4:4-6 when he pleads for moderation, joy, and thankful dependence on God.

The way we think and act—our own everyday attitude—is what emphasizes the mountains or valleys in life. It's mostly in the stroke of the brush as to whether our picture of life is good or bad—and we hold the brush.

The Roc's Egg Complex

Many problems confront us in our world today, and not a few of these exist because of a consuming complex. One of these might be referred to as the "roc's egg complex."

What is a roc's egg? No doubt one of the reasons you are reading this chapter is to find out.

There is a story from *The Arabian Nights* that tells of a very wealthy man who owned a lovely palace he was most proud of. One day a friend visited him and was given a royal tour of the beautiful palace. When the tour was completed, the friend remarked that the palace was almost perfect and that it lacked only one thing—a "roc's egg" hanging from the ceiling. Naturally, the owner did not know what a roc's egg was nor how to purchase one. Thus the magnificent palace that had brought so much contentment became a virtual prison simply because the owner wanted something he did not have, even though he knew nothing about the item he desired.

We immediately realize how terribly foolish this man was, and yet how many of us are miserable because we do not have something we are told we should? Sometimes we don't even know exactly what we desire, but we keep looking for something and just cannot be content until we find it.

How many of us are waiting until we find that "roc's egg," bringing on our own suffering, before we settle down to some important task before us, or until we begin to enjoy the blessings God constantly bestows upon us. "But godliness with contentment is great gain. For we brought nothing into this world, and it is certain we can carry nothing out. And having food and raiment let us be therewith content" (I Timothy 6:6-8). "Let your conversation be without covetousness; and be content with such things as ye have, for he hath said, I will never leave thee, nor forsake thee" (Hebrews 13:5).

How many of us are miserable because we don't have something we are told we should?

How wonderfully happy we could be if we could learn to follow the teachings of these verses: to live such a godly life as to appreciate God's continual presence, to so use our blessings as to fully take pleasure in them, and to allow these blessings to serve their purpose in our lives. Applying ourselves to the realization of these goals will prevent any "roc's egg complex" from making a prison of the free, happy, busy, purposeful, and useful life God intends for us to enjoy.

Slow Bicycle Race

One of my sons attended his first school in the Bermuda Islands when we were there doing mission work. During the school year, there was a day set aside as "Sports Day" which included soccer games, relay races of all sorts, mothers races, fathers races (and, I must admit, I came in second place in such a race competing against several nationalities of men), and a slow bicycle race. The object of this last race was to see who could ride the slowest without falling or putting one foot on the ground. The winner was the one who could keep his balance the longest while moving the shortest distance.

The slow bicycle race was most amusing, to the participant and the spectator! It reminds one, however, of many people in modern society. In the realm of civic affairs, religion, and practically every other worthwhile area, we find the counterpart of the slow bicyclist. Many try to see how slowly they can move and how little they can accomplish while still staying in the race. Still not content, some bring distress to others by trying to slow down the progress of everything and everyone else who wants to do good and go forward.

Anyone who has ridden a bike knows it would require more effort and balance to sit or move slowly, despite going nowhere, than it does to "move on." To better understand, envision a person on a bicycle twisting, turning, and leaning in every direction—all the while accomplishing nothing.

Any member of our society who tries to do as little as possible, assuming very little of the load, has to twist, turn, try to cover up, and hide. What is the worth of this effort? It can only bring anguish to everyone involved.

It is much harder for a Christian to keep his spiritual balance this way than if he is an active worker, going somewhere and accomplishing something for the Lord. The same basic principle is true in government at all levels and in civic affairs and any other effort to do good.

Solomon writes, "Whatsoever thy hand findeth to do, do it with all thy might" Ecclesiastes 9:10. The good people during Jesus' personal ministry said of Him, "He hath done all things well" (Mark 7:37). He earned this compliment by putting His heart into His work: by sharing His ability and showing a genuine, working interest in people and good things.

Wouldn't it be a most desirable goal to take advantage of our opportunities and meet our responsibilities so that we can one day have it said of us, "He did all things well."

Despite Failures, the Stream Moves On

A stick may be caught on a rock or a land mass as it drifts along, but the stream flows on.

An idea may never work out, a dream may never come true, a goal may not be achieved, and many plans may go unfulfilled, but the stream of life flows on. We can stop when the plan doesn't work or die with our dreams, or we can go on with the main stream of life and hope better things lie ahead. Perhaps there's something around the next bend even more worthwhile. Maybe the future holds something better because we have been tempered and prepared by failures and disappointments. A deeper sense of appreciation is often developed by some experiences not working out our way.

When we lose a loved one, it is difficult to face the regular tasks and responsibilities of life, but there are others to love and other matters that can still be very worthwhile. After suffering a great career loss, it may seem almost useless to keep on trying, but we can determine to learn and profit from even the worst things that happen to us.

Let us determine to never be caught up in fear, discouragement, pride, or even self-satisfaction and let life pass us by.

Opposition has often given birth to success. Goals have been reached just because someone was determined to overcome obstacles. What inventor has never faced a series of failures before his dream was fulfilled? How many have met with success every time they tried?

Opposition has often given birth to success.

The Lord's church had its beginning in the midst of adverse surroundings. Her first members had to "come out from a perverse and crooked generation" (Acts 2). These same souls suffered persecution from their first obedience. Christians were forced to leave their homes and loved ones (Acts 8). Yet, during this same period, the church experienced some of its fastest growth.

The Apostles were persecuted and opposed practically everywhere they went. Suppose they had faltered out of fear and quit their work because of perils and problems. Had they done so, God's plan would not be available to us, and without the hope it produces, life would hardly be worth living.

As the stream of life flows on, let us move with it—ever onward toward an eternal port, unhampered by the trials and tribulations that would block our efforts for good and our success.

Self-Inflicted Suffering

It is not unusual for people to place themselves in positions that produce self-inflicted suffering.

A very dear friend was told by her doctor if she did not quit smoking she could not live to be forty. After several years of health problems, she quit – but not smoking. She quit her doctor and ended relationships with many friends who diligently had encouraged her to break her life-threatening habit. She and her husband borrowed money from friends, money they seldom repaid. When friends would no longer help them support their tobacco and beer lifestyles, they refused to remain close to these friends.

Just a few years later, she called me long distance about midnight and began a heart-breaking conversation. Her first remark was, "Jack, I don't believe in God anymore; does that shock you?" I tried to convey that I was not shocked but sadly disappointed. She proceeded to inform me that if there was a God, He would not have allowed her and her husband to get in such a poor state of health. I reminded her that she couldn't blame God because her doctor had warned her of the dangers if she chose to continue to smoke. This point caused her attitude to mellow. After this phone conversation, though, I never heard from her again. Soon after, I learned of the untimely, though expected, death of the couple. Contrary to God's love, doctors' advice, and the loving care of friends, this couple brought on their suffering, and their death, by abusing their God-given bodies.

I have observed two attitudes of those in hospitals toward their care givers. One type complains about everything and never expresses gratitude for any service. Others are grateful for each effort made to make them more comfortable and meet their needs. No doubt you can guess who will receive the best care.

A dear little nurse expressed concern to me for inflicting pain as she applied pressure on an artery that was hemorrhaging. I assured her that I knew she was doing her job, and I was grateful for her efforts to save my life. The rest of the time she was my nurse, she was most caring and helpful. My actions and words towards her made my time in the hospital more pleasant. Much of her attitude was a direct reflection of my attitude.

It has also been my observation that patients who had confidence in their physician and faith in God healed more quickly and completely in many cases. The will to live, to get well, may well cure as many as the best doctors. Let us never forget to give God credit as well as our doctor. All of these factors, properly applied, can help make pain a friend rather than a foe.

A few years ago I observed people trying to fly a kite on the beach at Gulf Shores, Alabama (where sections of this book, including this one, were written). They were completely unsuccessful. The second day, the kite flew freely and with little effort. The difference was the cooperation of the wind on the second day. The situation brought to mind a statement made by John Neal: "Kites rise against the wind, not with the wind."

Paul writes, "When I am weak, then am I strong" (2 Corinthians 2:10). Great people succeed by dealing with and overcoming obstacles and suffering, not by complaining and giving in or giving up. Compare those who make it to the Olympics. Every one of them was willing to sacrifice and suffer, though still taking care of their bodies. The glory of winning for self and for country was preceded by much pain and suffering. The winners were repaid; the quitters lost the glory.

It is literally possible to worry oneself sick. Usually this is unmerited, unfounded worry and fear. Honest people freely admit that most of the things we worry about never occur. However, the self-inflicted pain of worry is just as real. If we can't help a situation, why worry about it? Find a way to harness that energy for good; every effort spent will occupy our minds and reduce time to worry. If we can help the situation we are worrying over, then we should do so, even if it causes us some temporary pain. During this hard time, it is important to remember that God knows what we need; if we seek Him, His kingdom, and His righteousness, our needs will be met (Matthew 6:32-33).

Attitude intensifies or diminishes our pain.

The Great Physician prescribes this attitude towards worry: "Take, therefore, no thought for the morrow, for the morrow will take thought for the things of itself. Sufficient unto the day is the evil thereof" (Matthew 6:34). Excessive worry today can truly weaken our ability to work out a problem, disturbing our rest and thus hindering the solution tomorrow. If we concentrate on the solution today, we are more likely to resolve it tomorrow.

❖ ❖ ❖

Much suffering is in our minds or in our effort or lack of effort for self control. Attitude intensifies or diminishes our pain. We cannot blame God for the way we use our minds or apply ourselves. Our body is designed to dispense waste; so is our mind. We must remove and replace the bad with good thoughts and goals.

When we choose to do evil, we miss out on the good results we desire. When we choose to do good, we may still suffer, but it will be for a righteous cause.

We inflict evil or discontent on ourselves by wishing for something we cannot acquire or do not need, envying those who possess what we think we need to the point of our detriment. We also bring hurt to ourselves and others when we possess a negative attitude, forget the future glory possible after our pain, and spend our time wrapped up in worry. The Hebrews writer recommends that we lay aside the weights that hinder us, exercise patience, and focus on good goals (Hebrews 12:1-2). Following this advice will help us avoid bringing needless pain into our lives and the lives of the ones we love.

Why Do Good People Suffer?

Why do good people often suffer as much as evil people? Is God fair in such cases? There are some basic reasons why good people suffer:

1) We are not perfect. As a result, our imperfections produce regrets, pangs of conscience, and natural painful results of body and spirit.

2) Satan already has many under his control; he desires good people as well. Job is a perfect example of this. See Job 1:6 and 2:1-10.

3) We are surrounded by evil. Sometimes this evil causes good people to suffer through no fault of their own; sometimes good people place themselves in positions of danger,

bringing suffering upon themselves based on their decisions.

4) Bad people and good people alike live in a world with laws. Even the mistakes of the good will produce consequences.

5) We suffer the consequences of the sins of Adam and Eve (Genesis 3:16-19, 22-24).

6) We must partake of new experiences or grow stale. We do not always know how to deal with the outcome of new experiences; since we are not perfect, we may choose to try the wrong experiences.

7) What is punishment to one may be a reward to another. For example, some people commit a crime to get in jail for the assurance of food, shelter, and safety. We still suffer the consequences of their crimes. God can bring good even in these bad situations. Some criminals find themselves, Christ, and salvation while paying for their wrongs. I know some powerful preachers who learned the truth of God's word while in prison. Some of these men are involved in prison minis-

tries, helping other people change their lives. Despite these good outcomes, the victims of those crimes, often innocent bystanders, still suffered.

8) Even good people fail to follow God's way. II Chronicles 7:12-16 records a case of God's conditional promises. Although these were the people of God, they could only escape some natural problems by meeting some God-given conditions. When they refused the conditions, they suffered the pain of disobedience.

Suffering of One May Bless Others

Some of the most successful, valuable people I knew, who were labeled handicapped by others, did not limit their capabilities for good by placing themselves in that group. I witnessed at least a dozen of these situations while my wife and I were with Freed-Hardeman University.

One of the best of the benefit dinner speeches at Freed-Hardeman was delivered by Gene Stallings, famed Alabama football coach. One of the most impressive parts of his message was when he provided some information about his special son, who was born with Down's syndrome. He said if he had an opportunity to go back and be given the choice of that son or a totally healthy one, he would have no difficulty choosing his actual son. Some would say that having Down's syndrome would bring nothing but suffering to the boy and his family, but Coach Stallings related several cases where his son had been a great inspiration to his family and other people.

We freely admit it seems unfair that one child should bear such a burden. However, rather than letting such things be a burden, some people decide to find the often hidden blessings. Others even turn out to be blessings to all who know them. Many of those referred to as handicapped are more determined to succeed, pushing themselves to lead an independent, full life of service and inspiring those around them by their determination.

Gene Stallings probably has been a greater influence and encouragement and will be remembered more because of his attitude and treatment of his family than his coaching ability. I am thankful we have Christians like this man. Every coach can't be overwhelmingly successful in his career, but with help, all can be Christians and accomplish lasting good.

✣ ✣ ✣

Some of the more valuable, memorable lessons have come from those who have suffered the most. The Apostle Paul is one of these great examples. Paul has given us more New Testament books than any other inspired writer. Job's story is one of the Old Testament examples of a man whose great misery blesses others through the lessons learned in its reading. While banished on the rocky isle of Patmos, John was commissioned to write the great closing book of the

Bible, Revelation. The suffering of these men, and their unique perspectives that were shaped by this suffering, continually bless others.

Some of the most valued books we read were authored by people who endured intense anguish. Their lessons of personal pain can make us more grateful and inspire us with greater determination to be better people.

Some of the best, most toucing worship hymns were written by Fanny J. Crosby. Many people who praise God with her songs may not know that she was blind. Her songs would be no more moving if she had lived with perfect sight. Regardless of her limitations, her hymns hearten and inspire people to this day.

Bob Spurlin wrote a most encouraging book titled *Don't Ever Give Up*. Bob, a talented, successful Gospel preacher, was stricken with multiple sclerosis in 1995. His sixteen-year-old daughter was killed in an automobile accident four days later. In spite of these heartaches, Bob continued to preach from a wheel chair for six months. During his affliction, Bob digressed from a cane, to a walker, to a wheel chair, and finally to a hospital bed. As the title of Bob's book suggests, he didn't give up. Using a voice-activated program, he created books that have blessed people in forty states and in seven foreign countries.

We do not know what this great man of God could have done had he been given good health throughout his lifetime; however, since he chose to continue to bless so many people despite his hurt, God empowered him to do what few perfectly endowed people have accomplished.

❖ ❖ ❖

It may well be that our personal pain can enable us to make a positive difference in the lives of others, sometimes those dearest to us and sometimes people we will never know. Would I be willing to suffer to make life better for a loved one? How much would I be willing to hurt to enable a loved one to go to heaven? (Philippians 2:20-21 shows that Paul was willing to make that sacrifice.) What would I endure for my child or my mate?

Our personal pain can enable us to make a positive difference in the lives of others.

Consider how much Jesus suffered to make our life better and our hope for heaven realized! Consider the connection between His love and suffering. I John 1:7 explains, "But if we walk in the light, as He is in the light, we have fellowship one with another, and the blood of Jesus Christ His Son cleanses us from all sin." Will we accept His gift, apply the blood, and allow His suffering to serve its purpose in blessing us?

Romans 8:17 explains that sometimes to be God's child, "heirs of God and joint heirs with Christ," we might have to "suffer with Him, that we may be glorified together." Serving the Lord, bringing His goodness to others, does not always require pain. Still, as tribute to both the power and love of God our Father, it is of vital interest to realize that God has the power to use the suffering of one to produce good for others.

Suffering of One May Save Souls of Others

Our first consideration of this idea may provoke our thoughts of Christ's bitter anguish for a part of His life, culminating in His cruel death on the cross. By His suffering the salvation of untold numbers has been made possible. The shedding of His blood was even essential for our salvation, for the chance of salvation for all people!

Another example I think of was brought to my attention in the mid 1950s. The daughter of some dear friends had married a young man whose parents literally hated the church Christ died for. However, the young man was kind, good, and open minded. With this attitude, he was converted by his dear Christian wife and his exposure to Christianity. This lovely couple had many of their dreams shattered when the husband was stricken with cancer. Fortunately, the man had already grown and matured enough in the faith to know that when he died there was still something far better beyond all the blessings of this life.

Visiting him often in the hospital, his parents became impressed that their son, despite facing certain death, showed no fear. Instead, he continued to talk about what he would say when faced with people like Moses, Abraham, Paul, and others in heaven. After watching their beloved son suffer and still maintain his faith and hope, they were forced to this conclusion: "That boy has something we have to have." As a result, once hardened souls were reached that could never have been saved by anything less powerful.

When I see the example of some so faithful today who, in spite of constant agony, are present for every worship service when they possibly can, I realize that they have given the Lord the right place in their lives. Almost every place I go in several states I see this situation; these people are a good example to those who are healthy and sometimes look for an excuse to miss this precious time of worship to the Lord and fellowship with others.

As we see such love for God and gratitude for being at worship, even through pain, we should take our blessings and responsibilities more seriously. For all who are blessed to serve, there are others who would love to be able, and still others who do not know God and the blessings we Christians enjoy.

Do I have the kind of life others feel they need? Do you enjoy such blessings?

Reasons for Suffering and Pain

We have attempted in our examination of this subject so far to use a common sense method in our approach. As we further pursue our thoughts, let us consider five very special blessings: our five senses. These I learned in my earliest years of education in a two-room country school.

The five senses let us see, hear, smell, taste, and feel. All are so natural that we often take them for granted. The fact is, if I can feel good I can also feel bad, and sometimes I need to feel bad in order to feel good later.

When a child touches a hot object, he may experience pain. At some time he learns a valuable lesson and takes care not to touch that source of pain again; this lesson often prevents a worse, most dangerous pain. A small burn on a finger could prevent a destructive burn to the entire body. Also, if the child could not feel the pain in his finger as he touched the stove, then he could burn himself beyond repair without the initial painful warning to remove himself from danger.

Our wonderful eyes provide so many pleasant visual blessings. As a result of the sensitive nature of our eyes, they have a very swift protective quality. A small particle of dust in our eyes can feel like a huge rock. The eye waters, a slightly unpleasant experience, to flush itself of something that might scratch it. As the sense of danger approaches, the eye will close in a split second.

Extreme pain is often prevented because minor pain has been experienced by the senses. Dr. Paul Brand and Philip Yancy have both said, “Thank God for pain” (Kippy Myers’ book *The Problem of Suffering* 118).

Some people do not feel normal pain; one might think at first that this is a blessing. I have personally seen cases in recent years that make me know Brand and Yancy were right in their view of pain.

One of the most admired friends and Christian brothers I know experienced damage to his body in the war such that one of his hands has no feeling in it. He could do much harm to that hand, such as cutting or breaking it, and cause long term problems without being aware by the warning of pain.

In the *Jackson Sun* in 2004, I read of a girl with a similar problem. Because of an untreatable disease called anhydrosis or CIPA, a rare genetic disorder, a five year old girl from Patterson, Georgia, felt no pain.

Her mother said that she would give anything for her daughter to feel pain. As we already noted, pain is there for a reason. In the mother's words, "It lets your body know something is wrong and needs to be fixed." She could not even sense extreme temperatures. Family and teachers had to watch her closely because she could be injured in a fall or other mishap and not even know it. She also could drink or eat something that was scalding hot, burning herself without even realizing it. Surely we can see from this example how pain can be a friend and a blessing.

❖ ❖ ❖

It is not at all unusual for a physician to inflict pain to heal or save a life. I have personally experienced surgeries ranging from the top of my head to the sole of my feet. Without some of those unpleasant experiences, including a triple heart bypass, I would not be alive today and enjoying more fully my Lord's rich blessings.

> Without some of those unpleasant experiences, I would not be alive today.

A young boy was brought to the doctor one day when I was there. He was a large, mentally-challenged young man. They had to send his grandmother out of the room. By sheer force, two nurses had to hold him down while the doctor gave him a necessary injection. He yelled as if the doctor were killing him, but no doubt the shot helped him get better rather than worse.

An early unpleasant experience of our daughter made her extremely afraid of all doctors. When she was about four years old, her mother took her to the doctor in Jellico, Tennessee. He examined her and said he had to give her an injection. When he left the room to prepare, my daughter told my wife, "Oh good, I won't have to take a shot." She was wrong. When it was all over, it took her a long time to get over the fact that her mother did not inform her that an injection and a shot were the same thing. It took many more years to sometimes request a painful shot to overcome a critical, long-lasting health problem.

One conclusion we must reach is simply all pain is not evil or even bad. God does not cause pain, but He may allow it to bring us to our senses, educating us and preventing worse torment.

Needful exercise may produce pain, but it results in good. Regular, proper exercise will bring positive results that can prevent many troubles. If we overdo our exercise, our bodies might hurt as a warning to slow down. God gave us a mind and senses designed to take care of our bodies.

We may endure pain to reach goals. Though unpleasant temporary pain exists, the end results may be very good. II Corinthians 4:15-18 is a divinely approved record of this principle. In part, Paul reminds that sometimes what is painful for the outward being is beneficial to our inward being. While the outward part is perishing, the inner part may be constantly renewed. Momentary, light affliction may bring about an exceeding weight in glory. Unfortunately, our outward vision, which is temporal, may not see the eternal results.

Pain May Produce Growth

When an older couple returned from a long mission tour, they were surprised to see a large crowd when the ship docked. They assumed the throng of people was there to welcome them. Elation turned to sadness when they learned the people were there for someone else. The precious, disappointed, aged minister turned to his wife and said, "I thought all those people were here to welcome us home." His sweet, wise, and discerning mate responded, "Honey, we're not home yet."

Many problems, disappointments, pains, and heartaches along the journey help us grow, preparing us for other experiences. Life doesn't end here nor even at death! Trials and pains make realized goals sweeter! Let us determine to enjoy the trip, but to always keep our eye on the destination, the ultimate goal. We must make whatever happens in life aid instead of impair us. We know an earthly trip will not place us on the road forever; we will someday reach our earthly destination, and it is the same with heaven. While writing this section of the book, I am sitting at the table watching the untiring waves roll in at Gulf Shores, Alabama. It is a difficult and exhausting drive to get here from our home in Tennessee; however, when we sit and enjoy this wondrous part of God's creation, we know it was worth the effort of the trip.

Trials and pains make realized goals sweeter!

We spent four years in the beautiful Appalachian Mountains when our three children were young. When we would start our 400 mile trip back to our parents' home in West Tennessee, before we even crossed the mountains, our children would be saying, "Are we there yet?" "How much further is it?"

We adults often express similar attitudes. Patience shrinks many problems, and experience reduces others to a small, acceptable size. While there are some bad experiences along the road of life, there are also some great men—men often made great by their hardships.

To some, worldly things become so attractive that we may almost forget our goal. If there were not some bumps along the highway, we would not appreciate smooth roads. If there were no pain and suffering, heaven would not hold such great interest. Would you leave all tonight to go to heaven? Let us always keep in mind, whatever happens, heaven will be worth what may be lost. Philippians 1:21-30 speaks to that grand thought.

While we are housed in this physical body, may we never forget the spiritual side of life! II Corinthians 4:11 reminds us that the spiritual is forever! As surely as we transfer our thoughts to more spiritual matters, we will have less material matters to worry about.

❖ ❖ ❖

Jumping to conclusions is not a good form of exercise. I receive many forms from doctors, hospitals, and my insurance company. The first glace is often very frightening. It suggests I owe from a few dollars to several thousand dollars. Then I am comforted by bold, black letters saying THIS IS NOT A BILL. At this realization, as I collect my feelings to a calmer realm, I am pleased to learn that the statement has already been paid. Before we lose our patience and sense of reasoning in life, we need to be reminded of the pleasantness of the bottom line: the debt of our sins has been paid!

How blessed we are to know that Christ paid our bill, if only we are willing to accept His conditions. I could never pay enough, but if I do accept my Redeemer, I will be richly rewarded. I love the precious old song by Elvina M. Hall: "Jesus paid it all; all to Him I owe. Sin had left a crimson stain; He made it white as snow." Jesus died that I might live (I Thessalonians 5:10).

Let me illustrate this point. A dying mother confided in her son, "I hope I have done enough." His comforting response was, "None of us has done enough, but Christ has." Our citizenship is in heaven (Philippians 3:20). Remember that! Though the journey may be painful at times, we are just pilgrims traveling through, on our way to a fairer land.

At one time in 2004, I noticed we had reservations for lodging in four places in four states. Most of these were on our way to another destination. Let us not confuse even our finest lodge or motel with our final home. If we do, unbearable pain will be ours eternally.

Why take any long trip with its unpleasant experiences included? We do so because of the desirable destination; however, the best here does not compare to our heavenly destination.

People who visit Freed-Hardeman University often hear 2,500-3,000 voices blended in praise to God. One visitor remarked, "This is the closest to heaven I will ever be." I hope it was an experience that took him closer to heaven: a foretaste of heaven itself. However, when God's people assemble in sweet fellowship to worship our Creator, it is for a few hours a week at most: our sweet fellowship with Christ and the redeemed of all ages will be unending. We need the good and bad here to develop the ability to appreciate the eternal blessings of eternal glory.

Why Do We Suffer?

Our suffering may often be attributed to our own chosen experiences. It is true that much pain is created by the actions of other people or outside forces; however, our own lives more often color our world, with our attitude toward sin often playing a major role. Attitude may be measured in one of three ways: we may love it, hate it, or be indifferent toward it. Even when we choose righteousness over sin, we may experience some degree of suffering. However, David's words recorded in Psalms 34:17-19 comfort us and make the pain of these times more bearable. He tells us that when the righteous call and the Lord hears, He delivers them. He is near to those with broken hearts, and those of a contrite spirit, and the Lord delivers these people out of their affliction.

On the other hand, God abhors evil and cannot bear to look upon iniquity. He loves us and hates anything that hurts us (Habakkah 1:13). When we compare our love for our children, our spouse, parents, or dear friends, we get a view of God's perspective. We strongly dislike anything that hurts these people and strive to protect or prevent it. That's why we say no at times to a child's request for something that we see could be detrimental.

We need to learn to hate sin, deal with it in our lives by putting it in its place and choosing another course. Even when we try our best to eliminate sin in our lives, we must be prepared for the certainty of its temptation.

A very dear friend expressed a cherished attitude in her prayers. Joy Baker said she would pray, "Lord, I know I have problems, but I'm not complaining. I need thy help. I'm thankful for all the good things."

If we become aware that we sometimes suffer because of our attitude towards sin, we can better avoid some amounts of pain. The more we focus on goodness, the less evil will appeal to us.

The Degree of Suffering Depends on How and Where We Build

Where we build and how we build our physical structures or our spiritual lives can often determine an amount of pain. It can also affect our failure or success.

Most who have read the Bible, even a little, have heard the vivid illustration recorded in Matthew 7:24-29. Christ compares the obedient to the builder who hears the instructions and erects his home on a rock. When the elements test this home, it does not fall because it has been built on a sold foundation. On the other hand, those who hear yet reject God's directions are compared to a foolish man who builds on the sands. When the elements come to test its strength, it falls because the sands cannot support it.

I had an opportunity to see a visual illustration of the Lord's well-chosen picture: as we stood on the edge of the Sahara Dessert, we saw an apparently modern structure. However, our guide told us the house was condemned. No one could enter because it was dangerous. A closer look revealed the wisdom of its condemnation. Huge cracks appeared in its walls because it was built on the sand.

Has the soil we are building on been tested? Heartache will follow if we do not meet the building code that is designed to protect us while building a physical structure. Much more so shall those suffer who refuse the guidelines of the Master Builder, Jesus Christ.

Some people bought a beautiful house in an attractive area. They were sadly disappointed when they learned the sewage system wouldn't work. This anguish could have been prevented had the contractor had the soil checked. He would have learned that it would not "perk;" it would not properly absorb water.

When we erect our spiritual house, we must exercise extreme care that where and how we build meets the Master's specifications. The wise and cautious builder of his spiritual house will not only hear the Lord, but will follow His unerring advice. When people heard the story we referred to in Matthew 7:24-29, they were astonished at His doctrine; He taught as one having authority. This voice of authority spoke the words recorded preceding those we already noted: "Not everyone that sayeth unto me Lord, Lord shall enter the kingdom of heaven, but he that doeth the will of my Father who is in heaven" (Matthew 7:21).

This statement further reveals that no feeble excuse will alleviate the pain produced by ignoring the proper authority. Take heed what you hear (Mark 4:24). Take heed how you hear (Luke 8:18). Hearing Christ with an attentive ear will determine the current and eternal course of your life. Pain and sorrow will be diminished as a result.

Money Related Pain and Suffering

The Bible contains more information on the use, and misuse, of money than on faith, repentance, confession, and baptism. There are over seven hundred direct references to money. Someone has said one out of six verses in the Gospel accounts deal with this issue. Two thirds of the parables contain lessons about money. Still, people often reject this vital advice, resulting in alarming situations and suffering because of improper respect for and misuse of money. We must recognize that God has a loving reason for providing so much material in His Word about the subject. No doubt we could eliminate much heartache by giving due regard to our loving Father's advice and guidance.

I would like to share with you a representative selection of money related references:

"But they that will be rich fall into temptation and snare, and into many foolish and hurtful lusts which drown men in destruction and perdition. For the love of money is the root of all evil, which while some coveted after they have erred from the faith and pierced themselves through with many sorrows." (Timothy 6:9-10)

"Give me neither poverty nor riches; feed me with food convenient for me; lest I be full and deny thee and say, Who is the Lord? Or lest I be poor and steal." (Proverbs 30:9-10).

"Moreover it is required of stewards, that a man be found faithful." (I Corinthians 4:2)

"The liberal soul shall be made fat." (Proverbs 11:25)

"He that hath a bountiful eye shall be blessed; for he giveth of bread to the poor." (Proverbs 22:9)

God says to His servant who gives acceptably that He will "open upon you the windows of heaven and pour out a blessing that there shall not be room enough to receive it" (Malachi 3:10).

Jesus says, "It is more blessed to give than to receive" (Acts 20:35).

Deuteronomy 8:17-18 tells us that God gives power to gain true wealth.

There seems to be more guiding encouragement for the proper use of money than condemnation of misuse. Note also that God promises rewards for wise use of our resources as well as warnings against abuse. Leading a life in accordance to these and a host of other references with monetary advice would surely prevent and even eliminate much pain.

❖ ❖ ❖

The love of money makes it an idol, and idols are always detrimental. The love of money creates thieves, robbers, gamblers, and liars. It causes its servant to misrepresent facts, neglect family, ignore responsibilities, commit acts of ill will or repute, cheat, hinder others, cause embarrassment, abuse friends, distrust, defame character, collect huge debts, disconnect self from blessings, and covet money (to name a few). In all these cases, money is a deadly enemy.

The proper use of money can make it a friend. If we allow the Lord to help us, we can turn a monster into a servant. Money can bring joy when we use it to help an unfortunate person or a good cause. Some of the most wealthy people I have known used their fortune to bless others through helping a friend with medical bills, establishing respectable businesses, starting a scholarship for deserving students, supporting missionaries, or simply buying a toy for a child. These actions are the only way to buy happiness. In such cases, money becomes a true friend. The smile of a grateful recipient can repay our investment; a good "thank you" is good interest on our gift.

Money can bring joy when we use it to help.

❖ ❖ ❖

Let it be known, though, that it does not require money to serve and give the most valuable possessions. Love is the most treasured possession: there is no substitute for it. Those who have been deceived into believing otherwise expose themselves to a multitude of the deepest pain.

My parents had very little money, but I would not exchange their love for all the monetary wealth in the world.

We may find it necessary to properly direct our love so that we can gain the most true and valuable treasure. Exercise care in determining where you place your love or what you fall in love with. Remember I Timothy 6:10 warns, "The love of money is the root of all evil." Love spent wisely and properly never quits rewarding us. Many of the blessings of true love never quit giving. Money cannot love you back. Material wealth perishes, but love will accompany us to a sweet eternal home. I Corinthians 13 has a statement that reminds us why we place our trust in love instead of money: love never fails.

Plenty or Poverty Can Produce Suffering or Satisfaction

It is possible to confuse plenty and poverty and so conclude that poverty is God's punishment while plenty is a mark of God's pleasure. Matthew 5:45 explains that the Father "maketh His sun to rise on the evil and on the good, and sendeth rain on the just and the unjust." Having money is not necessarily God's blessing, just as having little is not necessarily God's curse. The fact is some with our estimate of poverty are not unhappy, and others with riches are miserable. Some wealthy people never find happiness, and they always want more.

Some are consumed with fear that someone will rob or hurt them for their money. For example, one man I knew who was very wealthy lived a life of misery because he was afraid someone would break into his house and take some of his possessions. He could not sleep well. Trusting no one, he was constantly changing his will and put his money in several banks. He refused to buy things that would have made his family more comfortable. This man suffered miserably because of his wealth.

Another family I knew had a nice, comfortable home, but when they were blessed with more money they built a huge, new house. A bad crop and a bad choice placed them in financial straits, and they lost the new house, returning to the former one. Having a lot of money did not ensure the stability of this family.

I shall never forget a dear poor widow in the first church we worked with. Our first Christmas, they gave us a money tree. I do not remember what those who had plenty gave, but I do recall vividly this woman's gift of a quarter and a pocket comb. She gave what she had and enjoyed the approval of her conscience. I feel confident she delighted more in her gift than those with plenty. I know for certain she brought much joy and gratitude to our family and to the Lord.

The Prodigal Son

One of the greatest lessons in the Bible is taught by a selfish, irresponsible young man. We want to visit the account of what is often referred to as the story of the prodigal son recorded in Luke 15.

This young man did not know how blessed he was until a selfish mistake lost him all he had. It seems he may have been several generations ahead of himself, qualifying as a member of the "me now" period. He wanted to enjoy the rewards belonging to his future right away. Wanting to answer to no one, he desired to escape to a far country where his father and others who knew him could not advise and restrain him. His actions, new-found freedom, and wealth placed with fair-weather friends who helped him spend his inheritance quickly.

When he found himself penniless, friendless, and utterly destitute in a land of famine, he got a job of the lowest form. Only when this Jewish boy, who had been taught that hogs were unclean, found himself living with hogs did the realization hit him hard: this was not what he planned or what he wanted. "He came to himself," verse 17 explains. Only at this point, the lowest of the low, did he realize how good he had it back home. In fact, he desired at this moment to simply be a servant in the home at which he was once partially master.

My son, Dr. Deryl Hilliard, and I both earned a degree in counseling. He later taught psychology and counseling at Freed-Hardemen University and counseled in a private service. My years of counseling as a minister and serving as Director of Placement at Freed-Hardemen served me well. Both of us learned by study and good practical experience that one cannot receive needed assistance until he recognizes a need, admits the need, and then seeks help.

I wish to inject a thought here that every one of us needs to stop and take a personal inventory, no matter what age or position we are in. Are we where we want to be? Are we on target? Do we need to change our course, raise our goals, or seek help? Help is available! It is possible that hearing the story of the prodigal son is just what we need.

As unlikely as it seems, this irresponsible, selfish boy provides one of the greatest lessons our world needs in responsibility. His experiences of great pride leading to a great fall changed him from a give-me-everything attitude to one of hope for a chance to be responsible, to earn his way.

His case definitely teaches us that pain and suffering can be the friend we desperately need, a resource to show us the error of our ways, and not our enemy!

This young man also teaches us that, when we realize we have made a mistake, we need to set up a good plan to mend our error. Many people help mold our lives: parents, friends, teachers, ministers, and almost everyone we meet. However, it is our personal, individual choices that help or hinder us. No excuse helps us! Luke 15:18 notes the prodigal's confession, "I have sinned," and his conclusion, "I will arise." He did not say, "Why didn't Dad come looking for me?" or "Why did Dad overload me with responsibility?" He might have even blamed his brother. And yet, not only did he admit his mistake and recognize only he could correct it, he also created and followed through with a good plan to do so.

It is our personal, individual choices that help or hinder us.

The increase in his maturity is visible again when his anxious, loving father runs to meet his son. His father's embrace and plan for a welcome feast and other rewards is heartwarming. At the same time, the son's reaction to his own homecoming is worthy of note. He fully accepts his responsibility and admits his sin against both his earthly and heavenly father, showing true repentance.

This total story provides great evidence of the truth of Romans 8:28, "All things work together for the good to them that love the Lord." All of the bad experiences of the prodigal son become a catalyst that produced such good results: a reunion; a higher level of maturity, respect, and responsibility; and many great lessons to those who read the tale.

Our heavenly Father stands in the same position to those who allow His guidance through the good and the bad as the father in this story—welcoming us into His arms with blessings and triumph after our worst and lowest defeat.

Faith and Suffering

Remember the three Hebrew slaves who refused to bow down to the idol King Belshazzar made. Daniel 3 records this intriguing account. These young men said that they believed their God would save them from man and the fiery furnace, but even if He didn't they would still refuse to bow down to another god. Their faith was not lost nor in vain. Yes, they suffered the pains and pressures of standing up against their peers, authority, and possible death, but they were delivered from the fire. Their deliverance was not the only blessing; the event made a believer out of Belshazzar.

Paul knew he would suffer when he became a Christian, and he did from the very beginning of his Christian experience (I Corinthians 4:11-13). He endured hunger, thirst, nakedness, beatings, and homelessness. He labored with his hands, was reviled, persecuted, defamed, and made the filth of the world. When we see the rewarding satisfaction he later received and how by God's grace untold numbers have been blessed by him, how thankful we are he was willing to endure pain for the cause of God.

God teaches us that His kingdom is more important than material possessions or desires (Luke 9:57-62; Matthew 6:33). When Jesus promises a great reward for our service, He not only mentions some great blessings but is careful to include persecution as a part of the package (Mark 10:29-30). The passage in Luke 9:57-62 reminds us that His kingdom is more important even than personal comfort and family.

Our hero Paul suffered mental, physical, and emotional pain but never complained. He continued to believe in the goodness and promises of God (II Corinthians 11:23-29). In II Timothy 4:6-8 he declares, "I am now ready to be offered."

"Faith is not built on sunny days. Faith is built on days when it is raining and you have no umbrella, but you can still feel the warmth of the sun," is something Valorie Watrum, age 32, said just a few hours before being killed by a drugged hit-and-run driver. Can you imagine what her attitude did for her grieving husband?

We lost a beautiful little girl on Christmas day over forty years ago. A dear friend comforted us by saying, "You will adopt another little girl who will bring you much joy and pleasure." We applied for adoption, and nine months later we got the daughter who has fulfilled our friend's statement.

Any prize or goal that is really valuable is worth working for. I learned that as a teenager. You might remember me mentioning earlier that I picked cotton; once I saved up to buy my family's first radio, a used, battery-powered Philco. It was worth all the painful, backbreaking effort when we could be entertained by our favorite radio program. How much more cotton I would pick if that was what my Lord asked of me in order to get to heaven. (I am thankful that is not a requirement.) One of my most favorite and beloved teachers in college, W. Claude Hall, expressed it like this: "All we have to do is live a faithful Christian life." Of course that presupposes the fact that one has to first become a Christian by obeying the Gospel of Christ, our Savior.

When we think God asks too much of us and we cannot understand why, we need just remember that if we could understand all of God's actions, we would not need God. He alone understands how valuable heaven is and knows how much we can bear and what is reasonable of us.

It strengthens our faith when we see good end results for those who attempt what seems to be totally unreasonable. II Corinthians 4:17 sums it all up: "Our light affliction which is but for a moment worketh for us a far more exceeding weight of glory." In verse 18, Paul reminds us that all we see is temporal while the unseen is eternal. The truly wise are working toward the eternal.

Grace and Suffering

It is most encouraging to realize how God's grace can prevail over the greatest problem, threat, or suffering. The result of these next few pages hopefully will make us aware of how our obedient faith can connect us to God's power, wisdom, love, and grace.

Frank Chessor has written a marvelous book titled *Portrait of God.* He reminds us of the traits of our Creator over and over: one such trait is how our Creator can dispense His grace through simple circumstances when weak, troubled humanity accepts His gifts properly.

Man's pain and seemingly insurmountable problems have always provided an opportunity for God to display His power and grace.

The hunger of crowds over 3,000 and 5,000 was satisfied by the two small fish and five loaves of bread with a bounty left over. The pangs of hunger were nothing compared to the powerful gift from Jesus (Mark 9:12-16).

Jesus asked for a drink of water from what appeared to be a most unlikely source, a Samaritan woman at Jacob's well. As a result, not only was His thirst quenched, but He met the spiritual thirst of a multitude of lost souls. As I drank from that same well while traveling in the Bible Lands, I was overwhelmed by the history of that special place and this story. John 4 records this use of God's grace to meet suffering humanity's need as He spoke to a woman deemed unworthy by most.

Some of His followers had experienced a disappointing day of unsuccessful fishing. After Jesus invited them to try again in a designated place, their faith and His grace rewarded them with a most successful catch (Luke 5:4-10).

An eight-year-old boy named Josiah became a king. At sixteen, he endeavored to bring his erring people back to God. He sought to return to the religion of David, destroying idol worship when he was twenty-one. After four centuries of neglect, he returned the Passover feast to its rightful place with his people (II Chronicles 34). Even the faithful youth can be an avenue for sharing God's grace.

The book of Ruth records the story of a Moabitess named Ruth who returned with her widowed mother-in-law, Naomi, after the loss of Naomi's son, Ruth's husband. Despite her loss, Ruth is later introduced to Boaz, marries him, and gives birth to his son who is recorded in the lineage of David and Christ.

Even though the book of Esther is the only book in the Bible that does not mention God's name, it presents another side of our Creator. A worldly king got rid of his wife and three years later chose Esther as his new queen. She and her uncle, Mordecai, truly loved God. Their relationship to each other and to God enabled them to save the whole Jewish race. Part of the plan put her life at risk; however, her brave act of faith saved her, her uncle, and her people while putting them in a prominent place in the heart of future generations. You may remember the beautiful challenge Mordecai makes to Esther: "Who knows that thou art not come to the kingdom for such a time as this?" (Esther 4:14).

Who knows that you or I may be here and suffer a while that good may result?

Mordecai's challenge raises the question, "Who knows that you or I may be here and suffer a while that good may result?"

At one time a little captive maid was used to provide advice to her captor that resulted in his healing from leprosy and his introduction to God (II Kings 5).

Matthew 26:69-75 records Peter's foolish denial of Christ resulting in intense pain. Despite his lack of thinking, he became one of the most remarkable servants of Christ. We still benefit from his writings and his part in preaching the first Gospel sermon in full.

Who does not remember the wicked Saul of Tarsus and the suffering he brought on the cause of Christ? Later, his suffering on the road to Damascus helped him to obey the very Gospel he had fought bitterly. God's grace helped him become the beloved apostle Paul, and we cannot measure the good this man has done (Acts 9:1-20).

The remarkable aged John, while suffering banishment on the isle of Patmos, was rewarded with the grace of God to write the last book of the Bible, Revelation (Revelation 1:9).

How wicked and vile would one have to be to not appreciate the suffering Jesus experienced in His horrible death on the cross? He lost a hard-fought battle with the prince of the world, but He won the war and made our victory over death, hell, and the grave possible through His grace. Thousands of years later, our anguish is defeated, and we can be a part of the glorious kingdom He promised to build. The four accounts of the Gospel and especially Hebrews 9:28 and 10:10 show how His grace, love, and power have benefited us in ways we could never repay! All He asks in return for saving us from eternal suffering is to obey Him and accept the suffering that may result for only a season!

These are but a sample of ways Jesus has used and still uses His qualities to alleviate our pain and suffering. How thankful we should be for God's precious revelation of His comforting, saving grace!

Some Ways to Look at Pain and Suffering: An Examination

When we become overwhelmed with pain and suffering, it might be a good idea to ask ourselves the following questions:

1) Will it make me better, stronger, or more helpful to others as I consider the suffering of Paul and Job (the duration and intensity and the marvelous outcome)?

2) Will it help me develop patience? The Lord told us suffering develops patience (James 1:3-4). Perhaps one of the greatest needs in the world is more patience.

3) Will it make me work harder to go to heaven?

4) Will it help me remove some of the hindrances from my life: things, attitudes, or feelings?

5) Will it strengthen me for future adversity or future problem solving? Perhaps in about 90% of cases it will.

6) Will it bring me closer to God? Consider David's prayer in Psalms 4:1. "Hear me when I call oh God of all righteousness! Thou has enlarged me when I was in distress; have mercy upon me, and hear my prayer." Paul writes that when we are weak, God is strong (II Corinthians 12:7-10).

Health and Suffering

Even good health does not insure freedom from unpleasant experiences. Why?

Sometimes the healthiest abuse their bodies, and later the bad results catch up. At times we may not be aware that certain foods or activities are detrimental even though, or because, we are enjoying good health.

Sometimes things designed to help actually hurt. Drugs that have not been tested well enough may be detrimental even though we are convinced it will improve or increase our health.

Strength in some areas may mask weakness in others.

Improper techniques or applications of exercise or vitamins, which are good for us when used properly, can be damaging.

What helps me individually may be harmful to others. All our bodies are different in some way. One friend who was benefited by a certain vitamin recommended it to me; I was convinced it was harmless and would also help me. A visit to my doctor revealed a problem: when he found too much of a certain chemical in my blood, we both began to seek a reason for this change. I finally remembered I had been taking this suggested vitamin that I thought would be helpful. It turned out I didn't need it, and it was actually harmful to me.

Our health can be linked to our suffering by bad, ignorant, or improper choices we make in relation to our bodies.

Suffering Because of Weather

Did you ever get miserably hot or cold? Have you ever wished you could control the weather and make it always comfortable or keep it from raining on your parade?

We all suffer discomfort and disappointment that is weather-related in all seasons whether it be summer's heat, fall's unpredictability, winter's cold, spring's allergies, or more.

Just suppose people could control weather conditions: it would be different in every neighborhood, every home, and with every person. Problems would be multiplied including troubles with our health.

I can illustrate the problems that would occur by another man-made problem.

When the idea for daylight savings time first began, we were living in Malden, Missouri. A dear friend of mine sold beauty supplies to shops in a large area of southeast Missouri. The time change was optional for each area of town. This posed a terrible problem for his schedule. One customer would be located in a town that elected to adopt the change; another town eight miles away did not change their time. He might call on a shop in one of those towns and lose an hour or be too early for his meeting in the next town. As a result, he would lose several hours a week waiting between customers or having to change his entire schedule. At times he would lose a half of a day simply because people regulated the time.

If we controlled the weather, very similar disrupting problems would be faced daily. It could be a certain degree temperature at home and several degrees hotter or cooler at the mall ten miles away. We experience enough problems dressing to agree with the weather report now; if we were all in charge of creating our own "perfect weather," everyone would have to travel with several changes of clothes. Also, our health would be highly affected by the unpredictability.

God makes the sun to rise on the evil and the good and the rain to fall on the just and the unjust (Matthew 5:45). His wisdom is seen when we realize that weather conditions would differ from house to house if we were in charge, which would not make anyone happy unless we simply stayed home at all times. A common sense reasoning and approach enables us to realize God's way is the best after all. He alone has the wisdom to best control the weather. "For the wisdom of this world is foolishness with God" (I Corinthians 3:19). We must also remember that some weather disasters are due to the fact that we live in a fallen world that is not perfect, not because God desires to be cruel.

The greatest, strongest people involve God's help and turn problems, even weather problems, into blessings.

Memory—Blessing or Curse?
Pleasure or Pain?

One of our greatest blessings is the precious gift of memory. Most of my books have devotionals, inspirations, or other stories emphasizing the value of our memory.

Many of our memories produce pain and recall unpleasant experiences; however, some of our longest lasting blessings result from pleasant memories. The older we get the more we cherish fond recollections of golden days, friends, and experiences. They are always in our memory banks ready to call up, remove from the vault, and enjoy again and again.

At the same time, none of us is free from disturbing memories of the past which may arise, even without any effort, to provoke unpleasant feelings. How marvelous it would be to erase these, to spend them like money for something we desire.

For reasons which our human mind cannot completely comprehend, we cannot separate the good and bad memories and remove one without giving up the other

Who among us would sacrifice the pleasurable, cherished memories to be rid of the painful ones? This question leads us to seek out ways to focus on and enjoy the good memories while fading the unpleasant ones.

> The older we get the more we cherish fond recollections.

First of all, the good become more valuable when compared to the bad. Secondly, the involuntary recall of unpleasant past experiences makes us more selective in the process of making future memories. Since bad memories produce displeasure, we want to reduce possible pains by making better decisions.

When hurtful memories flood our thoughts like a constant movie that may be difficult to turn off, we should try to remove it by simply playing the good memories until they drum out much of the unpleasant past. Like counting our blessings, we can learn that the good outnumber the bad.

Indeed, memory helps us to plan a more satisfying and productive future.

What do we do when we get a bad taste in our mouth? We rinse our mouth out and refresh its feeling. We may do much the same with unpleasant thoughts and memories.

If the need is present, ask forgiveness for past sins that may haunt your mind. Develop new habits. Change your lifestyle or the company you keep. Our minds and bodies possess many common traits; the body eliminates waste, so can the mind. Healthy food creates a healthier body. Healthy mental food, likewise, creates a healthier mind. Norma Zimmer of the Laurence Welk Show has said, "Bitterness only hurts the one who is bitter." The attitude we harvest will affect our memories: bitterness will bring bitter memories, poor life choices will bring poor memories, and a life of goodness will bless us with good memories for a lifetime.

Some Wise Things to Remember to Avoid Suffering

1) Before signing a contract, remember, the large print may offer big advantages, but the wise person reads the small print to count the cost or risk.

2) Remember when you enter any contest, someone will win while others will lose. Be sure you can accept the loss before entering the game. Prepare well, plan wisely, apply yourself, and use your skills. Only then can you pray for the best outcome.

3) Some who think they have won often have really lost when they realize what winning can cost. Some are sad and feel they've lost only until they learn that losing really brought them something better.

4) He who waters the flowers and not the weeds will be pleased with the choice and the results. If we choose to dwell on the weakness of another and refuse to see the good, we will never be satisfied with any companion or happy with any choices.

5) One may view an old piece of furniture or pottery and pronounce it junk; the trained eye may see a priceless antique or treasure. One may look at an older person and judge him or her an old fogie or a useless being. The wise person may see a wise, experienced, mature individual and a priceless source of good advice and information.

6) We all have a body, mind, soul, and spirit. The spiritual part must be in charge now to insure our best eternal destiny and our best earthly harmony. Sometimes in order to possess harmony someone has to change. Use God's standard to determine who needs to change. If I am the one who needs to adjust all who know me will be blessed for my role in producing harmony.

Good Deeds / Gratitude: Pass It On

Quite often my memory presents me with a thought of what my godly parents sacrificed for me. Age makes me think more often, more seriously, and more thankfully for their good lives and the standards they set for themselves and for me. These thoughts not only evoke gratitude, joy, and pride, but they are co-mingled with a sense of indebtedness. How could I ever repay those who have gone before for all their expressions of love? I can't say thanks now or return those blessings!

The thought keeps pressing me: pass it on! Follow the example of those you admire. Indeed I would be a despicable ingrate if I did not follow my dad's example as he followed the Lord. He always did what he could to help others, often spending hours of time and sacrificing of his own comfort and resources. I must ensure that his example lives on.

In the small, loving community where I grew up in West Tennessee, there was an expression: “returning a favor.” Sometimes we say, “One good deed deserves another.” I thank God that marvelous motto was instilled in me. I hope I can share the blessings and joy that have been mine and my immediate family’s. The rewards of lifestyle can be immeasurable, and the results will long outlive those who practice it!

The practice will uphold good family names and carry over to those we influence.

The rewards include turning memories that produce sadness into gladness; gaining the special feeling of helping others, seeing the results for them, and seeing a smile or hearing a sincere “thank you;” possessing the knowledge that we did not rob ourselves of opportunities to help others in an effort to pass on the good deeds done to and for us; and achieving the reward for our good deeds not only in this life but eternally.

Why Others Subject Us to Pain

It is very obvious that many of our unpleasant experiences are inflicted upon us by others. Why would anyone elect to cause pain to another?

In many cases it becomes obvious that ignorance on the part of one may cause pain for another. One approach to healing is to figure out how we can help the unfortunate soul who hurts us through misunderstanding, bitterness, or ignorance. If our search is successful, we have blessed at least two people and likely many more. This is exactly the approach the One who suffered for us would have us use.

Perhaps the offending party has not seen the proper example. What a blessing it could be for us to show him or her that needed example. Some of the most valuable work of the true Christian is being an example and a good influence for one who needs it. The great apostle Paul didn't just follow Christ on good days or when it involved working with those who were kind, and Paul recommends that we follow him even as he followed the Lord (I Corinthians 11:1).

At times, one who inflicts suffering on others does not know how to bless those he or she loves and needs our example. Some of my best friends through the years started out by inducing a bad experience. When I accepted them despite the poor first impression, I was rewarded with a good friend.

Experience has taught me that many times the one who inflicts pain on others is experiencing disappointment or suffering themselves.

When Lola and I were looking for a place to live for our time in Bermuda, we visited one real estate office where the lady was very hateful. It was difficult to comprehend why one whose business was helping people could be so abrasive. When we left the office feeling disappointed and abused, Lola commented, "She has a problem herself, or she would not have acted as she did." I agreed this was a very reasonable deduction. A few days later, we noticed the sad story in the local paper of the lady's death. Having obviously wanted to end her miserable life, the lady shot herself. No doubt she had been living with a heavy burden. We learned that when people hurt us, they are likely experiencing some terrible suffering. There will be times when we recognize a call for help and can possibly supply a need. We turn our

Some of the most valuable work of the true Christian is being an example.

pain into good for the fellow sufferer and good for ourselves when we take such action.

How will some of our fellow travelers ever know about the source of healing available in Christ if we do not share the blessing of our knowledge? Some will refuse our efforts to help; in those cases, we are still rewarded with the knowledge we tried to ease their burden. In many instances, we will enjoy the greater reward of gratitude for our blessing.

Living with Suffering

I know of no one who has not experienced pain and suffering; it is a normal part of living. Obviously some suffer more than others. It is also true that some control or handle the pain better than others.

It is only normal that we be concerned about this uninvited guest, and also that we wish to eliminate it or deal with it in the best possible way. Even the great apostle Paul endured a "thorn in the flesh" as noted in the account of his painful endurance in II Corinthians 12:7-10. Paul took his problem to the Lord, imploring Him to remove the thorn. Referring to the pain as "the messenger of Satan," he did not blame the problem on God! The Lord's response was, "My grace is sufficient for thee: for my strength is made perfect in weakness." Paul's acceptance of this situation is most encouraging: "Most gladly therefore will I rather glory in my infirmities, that the power of Christ may rest upon me.

Therefore I take pleasure in infirmities, in reproaches, in necessities, in persecutions, in distresses for Christ's sake: for when I am weak, then I am strong." This great servant of God realized that the Lord would not only help him, but He would also enable him to use his suffering for good. If we allow God to help us turn our pain into service to Him and others, it makes it much easier to bear. When I concentrate on service, it seems to reduce my problems.

As strange as it may seem, the realization of others' pain is one way of helping us cope with our own. A visit to a hospital or nursing home will reduce our pain as we realize our blessings and help those who are hurting.

In II Corinthians 11:23-27 our brother Paul provides some additional help: he provides a lengthy list of sources for intense suffering. In verses 28-30 he shows us that much relief came when he concentrated on the suffering of others whom he dearly loved.

Many people seek a reason for hurt, and wise folks look first at their own lives for answers. As surely as we do, many times the cause becomes quite obvious. It becomes easier to discover ways to remove or reduce the problem when we first diagnose the reason. If something we have done is the cause, we must make steps to resolve the issue and avoid it in the future to reduce our pain. Guilt is one way to figure out the cause of suffering; if we quit the cause of our guilt, we can work towards removing the self-inflicted pain.

It is true that others often contribute to our unpleasant circumstances or experiences. That recognition provides options to deal with the problem. In some cases, we elect the extreme and simply cease our fellowship with the offending party. In other cases, we may choose the opposite extreme of making friends with our enemies. We usually find that their own problems cause them to be disagreeable. They may be crying out for help and be in need of our assistance to deal with some burden. Helping those who hinder us is one of the best ways to make friends and remove pain for at least two people. It is difficult to dislike one whom we pray for and determine to befriend.

This lesson was really brought home to me by my son, many years ago when he was just nine years old. For several weeks he claimed to be ill every morning to prevent going to school. After a time, his excuses ceased, and he was ready for school each morning. We finally were able to solve the mystery when he told us a bully was making his life miserable. When we asked how he resolved the problem he said, "I made a friend of him."

Suffering is inevitable; helping others through our suffering invaluable.

Quick Tips for Long Lasting Results

Our Dependable Father

When bad things happen, remember God can make it all work out for our good. He can also still provide hope for better blessings eternally.

Source of Rewards

Those who choose to serve Satan and hurt others will receive the reward of Satan and eternal punishment for their evil deeds.

Power of Forgiveness

How can we know the power of forgiveness unless we have both forgiven and been forgiven? It lifts burdens and heals pain in both these practices. If we have difficulty forgiving, we must remember Jesus on the cross looking down on His evil enemies that placed

Him there and hear Him say, "Father, forgive them." It should be easier to forgive.

God's Goodness

How can we know the goodness and love of God until we claim and accept it after pain produced by our mistakes?

Friendship

We cannot experience the value of true friendship unless and until we have both been a friend to someone who needed us and benefited from such friendship when it was badly needed.

True Friends

We never reach a place where we do not need God. However, we do not need those so-called friends.

Personal Responsibilities

We are responsible for the consequences of our own choices, good or bad. However, we must realize we are only responsible for the choices and consequences of others when we contributed to those choices.

Value of Pain

It's worth much pain and heartache if we gain something worthwhile and become a better person. When pain comes, look for the possible good that may result.

Include God in Plans

Remember, if we can't make God a part of a plan, we must forsake that plan.

Seek Help

Never attempt to resolve any problem or pain alone. First seek God's help; next find a trusted and experienced friend to confide in for help.

Help from the Lord's Plan

Remember that Jesus never lost sight of His goal and His Father's plan for Him. This devotion made it easier for His human nature to successfully deal with His suffering.

Never Blame God

Rather than blame God, we must seek His help. He is never responsible for our pain, but pain never becomes so great that He cannot help His child. Depend on Him, be patient, and don't expect the answer to always come in the way we expect.

Help

No one can know exactly how we feel or when we are hurting, but true friends can always help if we ask them.

The Cost Involved

Most lessons cost something; pain may be the price, but it may also become a valuable investment.

Inventory Pains

Take inventory! Are the material possessions that seem so precious worth all the concern, pain, worry, and hours of work we invest to possess them? Are we inviting pain for a few years, days, or hours of pleasure?

A Need to Change Goals?

Can we eliminate suffering by changing our goals and priorities? Are we risking health for just material, temporary treasures? When we realize a need for change, we must act immediately.

A Plan that Always Works

Remember to always seek God and His righteousness first. That plan will eliminate many heartaches! Remember God is not limited; however, our getting in the way of His plan or putting our goals above Him will hinder us.

Reputation

Determine to make no choice that will hinder our reputation! A good reputation helps prevent much pain and provides needed help at other times.

Resist Satan

Never let Satan get his foot in the door. That is like inviting him in. Resist his every attempt to compromise (I Peter 5:8-9).

Pain Can Be Like Money

Pain can actually be like putting money in the bank. The time may come when we can withdraw the interest (personal experience) gained from it.

Help Provided

When our hands are tied, our hearts are heavy, and our eyes are blinded by tears, God can provide the hands, hearts, and eyes of others to help if we are His children.

Attitude

A huge percent of healing is a result of having the proper outlook. Our attitude toward God accounts for much of our attitude toward other people and circumstances.

Sensitive toward Others

Our own pain makes us greater servants of our Father because it enables us to be more sensitive and helpful to others. We can never sympathize and empathize with others unless we have experienced what they have endured or are enduring. Remember those who have been where we are can help us in troublesome times. Jesus has been there, and so have other good people. They can and will help!

Jesus Has Been Where We Are

When calling on the Lord in times of distress remember, when He was on earth, He grew hungry, thirsty, and tired. His friends failed, denied, and betrayed Him. He had enemies. He lost loved ones to death; He saw loved ones suffer. People lied about Him, and many rejected His advice and help. He did physical labor and walked hundreds of miles. Suffering one of the most painful deaths possible, He did it all for you and me. When we consider all this, it makes our faith easier and stronger. He hurts when we hurt. He understands our every heartache, and He paid the ultimate price to earn and deserve our faith. He is ready to help when our need and faith lead us to call on Him.

God's Promise

"I will be with you." (Genesis 26:3, 31:3, 39:2-10, 39:20-23, Joshua 1:5, Isaiah 4:10, Jeremiah 1:8, 15:20, 30:11, 42:11, 46:28, Haggai 1:3, 2:4, I Samuel 16:18, and I Samuel 18:24)

Our own personal experiences will bring all these to life and see us through the worst of times.

New Testament References to God's Promise

God says, "Be not afraid" through the Angel to Zachariah regarding the birth of John the Baptist (Luke 1:13), to Mary (Luke 1:30), to the shepherds (Luke 2:10), to God's flock (Luke 12:32), and through Jesus to the disciples (John 14:27).

Paul in all his strength said that sometimes he experienced fear and trembling in I Corinthians 2:3, but in Acts 18:9-10, "Then spake the Lord to Paul in the night by a vision, 'Be not afraid, but speak, and hold not thy peace; for I am with thee, and no man shall set on thee to hurt thee, for I have much people in this city.'" The Lord promised him personal help and help through His people. He will do the same for His faithful servants today.

Faith and Deliverance

Anyone familiar with the Bible knows God never fails to keep a promise. If we examine the many promises God made through Bible history we are strengthened to learn God has always kept His word; there is no reason to believe He will fail to save those who will accept His grace by obedient faith.

How many fears can be allayed or pain and suffering prevented if we take our all-powerful Creator and Father at His word!

As we examine case after case of those who heard God's promises, we can find comfort in the stories of those who suffered but were blessed by following God's direction. When we give due consideration to all these examples of promises kept despite difficulties, Romans 8:28 takes on a new and refreshing meaning: "All things work together for good to those who love God and respond to His calling."

David's Psalms are filled with his cries to God for help in trials and his gratitude to God for answering his prayers. When David wrote his often quoted twenty-third Psalm, he did not speak of avoiding a walk through the valley of the shadow of death, but he did say the Shepherd would walk with him. This is comforting evidence again of the Lord's interest in our deep trails and His readiness to assist and deliver us. Jeremiah expressed it like this: "It is the Lord's mercies that we are not consumed, because His compassions fail not" (Lamentations 3:22).

When enemies seem to be as big as Goliath to a young boy, remember God is in there to fight for us too. The beautiful book of Revelation closes God's inspired message to His people with the assurance of victory for the faithful. This guarantee makes it easier to fight life's battles no matter what form the enemy takes.

God's love for us is clearly illustrated in the special account of the prodigal son in Luke 15. When this erring son returns to a loving father with a penitent spirit and confesses his foolish mistakes, the father accepts him back and begins to shower blessing upon him. The Lord uses this story to help us understand what our heavenly Father is like.

Our God is indeed the Father and Author of Comfort. What a blessing it is in times of distress to realize what our Creator is like; He knows every little detail about His children.

Delivery and Victory beyond the Physical Realm

We have spoken of the victory in Jesus emphasized in Revelation; it is essential that we consider what that victory really entails. One of the world's major religions today offers only physical rewards to those who serve their own agenda. They make satisfaction of those lustful desires so complete for those who buy into this cause that many are willing to sacrifice their lives to gain promised immediate entrance into "their heaven."

God's word makes it clear that there is a judgment in between this life and the better life (Hebrews 9:27-28). After that, the faithful Christian enters into a state totally free from all the troublesome physical pleasures and lusts that create so much pain in our current present world. The eternal spirit enters an abode not made by men's hands but by God. The spirit is freed from anything that causes pain and fear. "For we know that if our earthly house of this tabernacle were dissolved, we have a building of God, a house not made with hands, eternal in the heavens" (II Corinthians 5:1). Note Revelation 21:27 says of heaven that nothing will "enter into it anything that defileth, neither whatsoever worketh abomination, or maketh a lie, but they which are written in the Lamb's book of life."

"If in this life only we have hope in Christ, we are of all men most miserable" (I Corinthians 15:19). We do enjoy a hope in this life in Christ, made obvious by many promises and also by personal experiences; however, that hope reaches far beyond this life with its good blessings and its pain and heartache. The best is not only yet to come, but it is eternal. Our Lord has provided assistance beyond human helps, to overcome the trials of the present as we plan and prepare for the best.

If we resist the devil and accept the grace of God, we can have eternal glory.

I Peter 4:12 reminds us that we can expect trials to accompany this earthly sojourn. In verse 19, the writer emphasizes that we can commit the keeping of our souls to our faithful Creator. In I Peter 5:7, he reveals we can cast all our care upon Him for He cares for us. In the very next verse, he reminds that the devil will be seeking an opportunity to devour our souls. He continues with the thought that if we resist the devil and accept the grace of God, we can have eternal glory by Christ Jesus, after we have suffered for a while.

To summarize, the devil—not God—will tempt us and create suffering. God's grace and guidance are here to help us overcome. By our own diligence and by accepting help from God, who is more powerful than the devil, eternal glory is available.

Pain and all things here are temporary. An all-powerful God stands ready to help now, and eternal heaven awaits the obedient child of God; the very thought makes pain and suffering more bearable and burdens lighter.

Remember well that Christ Jesus suffered intense pain so that we could be removed from all pain in a better, eternal state.

When the Lord commissioned John to write the great book of Revelation, he wrote to seven churches of Asia (Revelation 2-3). All of these had problems that placed them in danger. However, they all were given choices and God's guidance to overcome those problems and enjoy great rewards.

A note should be made here about misplacing our values. Some of humanity's biggest problems with pain and suffering are a result of attaching more importance to physical and material valuables than to spiritual values.

A great cause of unhappiness and feelings of need is when we attempt to satisfy spiritual needs with physical things. No matter how much we cram into our physical bodies, nor how important we think our physical desires may be, we sometimes let spiritual needs go unsatisfied. Health and happiness require that the needs of our whole being must be fulfilled.

We are subjected to pain, suffering, temptation, and a host of other difficulties, but God has provided us with choices and guidance to overcome these difficulties with the hope of heaven.

Desired Happiness Can Lead to Misery

Our search for happiness often leads to misery. How is this true? Because our search for happiness frequently leads us on a quest for material things. We may actually accumulate a heavy load of luggage that burdens us down, rather than lifts us up—that draws us away from a goal rather than enabling us to reach it. The desires of the flesh (body) are so powerful they can demand too much of our attention. The result can lead to starvation of spirit and soul.

Solomon tried all the sensual desires: power, beauty, prestige, wealth, and even earthly wisdom. One would think his notable wisdom would direct him to the true source of his happiness; however, we see his admission of failure and consequent misery. He gave us the results of his experiment with the physical in Ecclesiastes 1:13-18 and 2:1-24.

Often seekers of happiness today search for satisfaction and fulfillment in material possessions, sexual fulfillment, honor, publicity, etc. This often leads to divorce, disease, prison, or poverty. All of these result in misery. What is the problem? Leaving out or leaving behind a basic need of other parts of our being—denying conscience, spirit, and soul.

"This illustrates the close connection between body and mind. When we allow outside force to infringe on the mind or body both are disrupted. In today's stressful world we can see why it is important to allow all our being to be respected and cared for. If we fail to control any part of our being we suffer ill consequences for all our being" (Hilliard; *Spirit Ritual* 114).

Locked Gates

When we were in the Bermuda Islands in mission work we lived in "The Old Homestead" on Middle Road in Devonshire. Quite often I walked to the post office, and I passed a small grocery store at the corner of Tee Street and Middle Road. There was a fence around the garden that joined the store, complete with a gate that was always padlocked. Despite the locked gate, however, one could easily gain access to the grounds because two panels of the gate were missing. I often thought that this represented well the life of many people.

So many of us are extremely careful about some things, while we are very negligent about others. That this characteristic has always been true of man is seen by the teaching of Jesus. Many times He voiced His disapproval of such inconsistency. He expressed this attitude in this unique way in Matthew 23:24, "Ye strain at a gnat and swallow a camel." Just before this quote He mentioned their care to tithe the small garden herbs of mint, anise, and cumin while omitting the weightier matters of the law like judgment, mercy, and faith.

How often we are diligent to guard against stealing or drunkenness, yet we fail to guard our tongue, and our speech hinders the cause of Christ and destroys our good influence. Certainly Jesus warned against stealing and drunkenness, but He also condemned the misuse of the tongue and the mind. Colossians 3:5-9 lists a catalog of sins and places lying and filthy speech in the group with adultery and idolatry. Revelation 21:8 places liars in the group of sinful men who will be lost. In James 2:10 we are told if we keep the whole law yet offend in one point, we are guilty of all.

Many make it a habit to study diligently, and no one doubts the importance of this, but Jesus also said the man who hears and does His word will be blessed (James 1:22-25).

Let us exercise all care to keep our locks in order and the panels in place as we strive to keep the devil out of our lives, protecting ourselves from this needless suffering.

Stand Up and Look Around

What is the very first thing one does when he falls down? It's just as natural as can be to jump up and look around to see if anyone is looking.

When one is down mentally or spiritually, he would do well to get up and look around also. Any time we are depressed and feel the burden of the whole world is upon us, all we need to do is look around and find someone else who is in far worse conditions. When we go to the physician or visit the hospital, we always see people that make us ashamed of our complaining and feeling sorry for ourselves.

There is another advantage in getting up and looking around. We can find someone who is interested in helping us. In many cases there is someone just waiting for an opportunity to help. We can benefit if we are willing to reach up and accept that help. Sometimes, however, we like feeling sorry for ourselves. We don't really want someone to help. On other occasions we just want someone to sympathize with our plight, but not to change it. The Bible teaches Christians to seek opportunities to do good (Galatians 6:10). Most often there is a Christian ready to lend a hand when we are down or depressed.

Still more important, the Lord is always ready to help. In the first place our problems are not any greater than those others have. I Corinthians 10:13 tells us no temptation has taken us that is not common to man. Next, the encouraging passage tells us God is faithful and will with every temptation make a way of escape. So as we look around we find others worse than we are, we find friends ready to help, and we learn there are scriptures in God's word designed to comfort and guide us. As we look up we see a faithful Lord who can and will help with any problem or temptation of life. "All things work together for the good of them that love the Lord" (Romans 8:28).

Religion Helps Determine Friends and Foes

Even religion has not escaped the allurement and entrapment of the giant of physical satisfaction, a temptation that often overshadows the rest of our fourfold being.

We do not deny that satisfying the appeals of the fleshly man brings pleasure. We can find examples in God's word that prove these are often temporary. Note the experience of Moses: "By faith Moses, when he was come to years, refused to be called the son of Pharaoh's daughter, choosing rather to suffer affliction with the people of God than to enjoy the pleasures of sin for a season… esteeming the reproach of Christ greater than the treasures of Egypt, for he had respect unto the recompense of the reward" (Hebrews 11:23-36).

It is easy to be blinded by immediate fleshly satisfaction and not look to the final goal of what we want: a lasting eternal reward, a durable and true satisfaction. Perhaps we need to let God's light shine on the future where our soul will dwell and not just the present where fleshly pleasure often drowns out and blinds our view of our home of the soul. God made us capable of developing a priority list that harmonizes the needs of spirit, soul, mind, and body. If we seek first the kingdom of God and His righteousness, the rest of our true needs will be supplied (Matthew 6:33). That is the clean objective of our being!

When our religious needs accept the false premise that worship must always satisfy the feelings of the worshiper—with pomp, ceremony, physical emotions, and other appeals of the flesh—rather than to the object of our worship (our God and Creator), we'll need to get our priorities in order. Only at the point when we recognize the true objective of our worship will we eliminate much of life's most bitter disappointments. How can we pray for our needs to be met when we reject the first condition God requires toward that end result? Our Father in heaven is the audience. It is not about what pleases us in worship but what pleases Him. Then and only then will our true benefactor meet our needs and answer our requests.

When we are in a position of need because of our destitute circumstances, we realize we must meet the requirements of God's condition. After all, He is the one in whom we seek relief and often the only one who can help. An all-wise God knows our needs and our all-powerful God alone can supply our most important needs. Indeed it is possible to become a slave to the very attraction we seek freedom from: our misery and pain. Only the One who made us knows our true necessities and exactly how to supply them. He always seeks our best interests, and we please Him when we seek what a true Father wants for His children.

We must realize that God works in His own way, but also in His own time frame. A good father is patient with his children, and he teaches his children to learn and practice patience as well. As we grow older, we begin to realize that patience is a valuable characteristic and a powerful asset. I understand now, as I have for years, that my parents did not immediately grant my every wish, but in good time, if it was in my best interest. I always received just what I needed. I know my heavenly Father works in the same best way for me! God has not always answered my prayers immediately nor in the way I expected. Later, though, I realized the need had been fulfilled in the very best way, and I have been grateful for the proper outcome.

Pain and Suffering in the Bible

If one goes all the way back to the first part of the first book of God's revelation to man we find the first answer to why we suffer. We already noticed immediately following the first sin of the first couple (Genesis 3:1-6) God reminded them of their changed condition, saying unto the woman, "I will greatly multiply thy sorrow and thy conception; and in sorrow thou shalt bring forth children" (Genesis 3:16). And unto Adam He said, "Because thou hast eaten of the tree I commanded you not to eat cursed is the ground for thy sake: in sorrow you will eat of it all the days of your life" (Genesis 3:17-18). Then God informed him there would be thorns and thistles and sweat involved in producing food.

As we examine God's new covenant we are told, "Wherefore as by one man sin entered into the world, and death by sin; and so death passed upon all men, for that all have sinned" (Romans 5:12).

How sad it would be if this inspired book ended on that sad note. We are blessed by a great hope extended in the same chapter. Verse 19 shows us that by one man's sin we all became sinners; on the plus side, one man's obedience made it possible for all to become righteous. The first couple's sin brought all its ill consequences. The obedience of Christ made possible our salvation from sin through His righteousness, if only we will obey.

❖ ❖ ❖

The Bible, God's personal prescriptive, directive for happiness, and help from sorrow, records many personal conversations with God. Our Father is always attentive to those who obey His will; we can talk to Him anywhere we may be. When we read His message, He speaks to us. He knows our needs before we ask, but He is pleased when we ask and follow His great plan. When our burdens become too heavy to bear, we must remember our strong, loving Father can never be overburdened. The fact is as we place our burdens on Him, He feels relief in our faith in Him.

The obedience of Christ made possible our salvation from sin.

If we feel there is any reason to doubt God's love, interest, and care or His power to help, we must simply read about His help for His children from Genesis to Revelation.

As long as His people were faithful, God provided food, water, shelter, comfort, and rescue from their most powerful enemies. He calmed the storm-tossed sea and stayed the water of the Red Sea for His beloved people. Does God love us less than He did those in the past? Is He less powerful and loving than He has been? Obviously one of the reasons for recording so many instances of His intervention on behalf of those throughout the Bible history was to reveal His power and love for His own.

We may not understand how God has worked in days gone by, nor do we recognize how much He cares for those who serve Him now. It is not ours to ask why, but what! What does our Father require of me to be included in His family and come under the umbrella of protection? The answer is found to that question for the honest, humble, obedient child today. The Father speaks through His Son; His Son has spoken to us in His written, inspired word (Hebrews 1:1-2).

When we read Acts 2, we note what people had to do to remove the heavy burden of sin and enjoy relief and communion with the Father. The rest of the book of Acts through Jude reveals His message of comfort and eternal salvation to those willing to accept His plan of relief. The closing chapters of God's letter in Revelation disclose the final result of our walk with our Lord; along the way we learn more about our prayer life and our attention to His guidance. The glorious Gospel tells of God's power to save both Jew and Gentile. It includes any one who renders obedience to the precious plan of salvation (Romans 1:16).

Through that beautiful message we learn how to get into Christ (Galatians 3:26-29). It also reminds that all spiritual blessings are in Christ (Ephesians 1:3). What a relief it is to know we can stay on speaking terms with our Creator. This powerful, loving Creator is always alert to the cries and pleas of His obedient children. God is never far from those who choose to accept His plan and stay close to Him (Acts 17:27, Hebrews 13:5). Burdens are lifted; grief, pain, and sorrow are left at the feet of our Father!

Just as God's people of every generation have met with opposition from Satan, we will too. We do, however, have the assurance that the God who made us and loves us is more powerful than our arch enemy!

Are we asking our Father to help us, and are we employing His plan to accept His help? If so, we have reason to enjoy the blessing of faith and its fruits. God expects obedient faith and rewards, comforts, and secures those who permit Him to be our Savior!

Prayer Is a Source of Relief

Where do the fortunate children go any time they hurt or have a problem? How blessed they are when they have loving parents to seek help from. The precious place of prayer, when life closes in on us, when problems are too big for us, when there is no one else to trust and depend on, is a very special gift from our Creator and Father. Even though we know the needs of our children before they ask, we still gain much pride and satisfaction when they ask us for help. How would our heavenly Father feel if He never heard our voice or if we left the impression we felt no need for Him? Matthew 6:8 tells us God knows what we need before we ask; He immediately gives us a model prayer, encourages us to ask, and reveals His pleasure in satisfying our legitimate needs.

Have we considered the fact that we honor our heavenly Father when we go to Him in prayer—because we are expressing our confidence in Him? We express our need for Him, our awareness of His being, and His special place in our life when we pray.

❖ ❖ ❖

The author's parents, who were always a source of comfort and wisdom.

Hope—Antidote for Pain

Hope is one of many aids for pain relief. Basically, anyone who loses hope becomes a servant of misery. On the other hand, as long as one has hope it is possible to conquer almost any foe. Hope can indeed turn the foe of pain into a friend of one in deep need. As long as hope remains we have an avenue of escape. In the absence of hope the iron gate to escape is securely closed.

How many battles, physical and spiritual, have been lost when all hope was gone! Contrariwise, how many victories are won because the faintest ray of hope was visible?

Many of us have read or heard about the soldier who seemed to be a hopeless victim of a lost cause. For some time he hid from his enemies in an old barn. One day he lay on his back looking up at the rafters in despair; he was feeling the pangs of loneliness and total loss. Suddenly he was attracted to a spider making desperate attempts to get from one rafter to another. Over and over it tried, only to fail. However, the lonely, desperate solider noted that the lowly spider never gave up. Each failure was met with another effort to reach its goal. Finally, after many defeats, it made it to the place it had failed many times to reach. That faint ray of hope shined in the soldier's befuddled mind. He arose and returned to battle. Inspired by new determination from, of all things, a small bug, he was enabled to succeed in his next effort.

The Lord used expressions like knowing "hope is an anchor of the soul" (Hebrews 6:19), wearing a helmet as "the hope of salvation" (I Thessalonians 5:8), and having "hope even beyond this life" (I Corinthians 15:19-20, Titus 3:7). And in Ephesians 2:12 the Lord places "without God" and "having no hope" in the same category. Hope is not possible without God.

The choice is ours to leave God and hope, one of our greatest defenses, and thereby lose the greatest of all blessings, eternal life. We also have the power to choose God, giving us access to an anchor, a protective helmet, and a hope of heaven. This hope for the future can bring comfort and become an antidote for present pain.

The Christian's Father of Comfort I

Many of us have experienced one of the deepest pains of all: the loss of a loved one either to death or in some instances Alzheimer's or other mental disorders. We may reach the painful experience of having no one to talk to. We may not be able to communicate to that loved one because he or she is no longer there, mentally or physically. There is no one else on earth, not even a closest friend, who can completely understand what we are experiencing. How desperate, how miserable, how lost we may feel!

However, there is never a time when a faithful child of God is alone! Our heavenly Father knows us better than a spouse, a child, or a parent. He is always available, ready to listen to our most pitiful pleas. He understands. He has the power and the love to help beyond any earthly assistance. I have personally reached the point where I was constrained to plead with God, "I have had all I can stand." At such times I soon received the help and relief I desperately needed. I knew my Father perceived the extent of grief or pain I could bear, and He made the burden lighter and bearable. I also feel every member of my family has found the heavenly source of strength, the One we can talk to when absolutely no one else is available or able to help us.

As age creeps slowly but surely upon me, I realize more and more how much my earthly parents sacrificed for me. The more I recognize that powerful truth the more aware I become of what my heavenly Father sacrificed for me. I know my earthly father would listen to my pleas, and my Father in heaven is even more powerful and more loving. One big difference is that I suffered the pain of losing my daddy, but my Father in heaven will always be there. This is another viable reason for becoming a child of God; God is always there when there is no one else to talk to, no one to understand my pain, no other ears open to my greatest needs and requests! "There is none like unto the God Jeshuron, who rideth upon the heaven in thy help, and His Excellency on the sky. The eternal God is my refuge and underneath are the everlasting arms: and He shall thrust out the enemy from before thee; and shall say, Destroy them" (Deuteronomy 33:26-27).

> There is never a time when a faithful child of God is alone!

It is difficult to imagine how anyone who reads that encouraging assurance could not realize there is help for every problem for God's obedient child. Note

II Corinthians 4:7-10, "Troubled on every side yet not distressed; we are perplexed, but not in despair, persecuted, but not forsaken; Cast down but not destroyed; always bearing in the body the dying of the Lord Jesus, that the life also of Jesus might be made manifest in our body." Jesus died for me, but He is now in heaven at the right hand of God. Trust in the Lord! Paul always believed that no matter what happened the Lord was there to help. We must always be aware of the death and the resurrection of Christ; He fully understands every experience we could ever endure.

Under inspired experience Peter writes, "Casting all your care upon Him; for He careth for you" (I Peter 5:17). Almost two thousand years after Peter penned those comforting words, Frank E Graff was inspired by his own pain to write a very popular song I still enjoy today. The title is "Does Jesus Care?" It contains the assuring phrase, "He cares; I know He cares." Hence in a very special way one man's pain resulted in the production of a source of comfort for other fellow sufferers. This hymn, growing out of God's own words, provides a needy prescription for mankind today!

"Thank you for the valleys, Lord, for this one thing I know! The mountain tops are glorious, but it's in the valleys that I grow" (Jane Eggleston).

Never forget!

If every Christian were killed, Jesus Christ would still be alive to keep His promise of heaven for the faithful. Herod did all in his power to kill the baby

Jesus. Untold numbers suffered loss and intense pain (Matthew 2:13-23). Still, Jesus continues to be a source of comfort to us all.

The Christian's Father of Comfort II

Beyond the veil of tears, storm-tossed sea, wars, host of foes, threats, pain, anguish, suffering, and physical death a loving Father looks down, ready to comfort, bless, and encourage us and finally to take His faithful children to a beautiful heavenly home.

What a source of comfort in times of distress to realize what God is like! He knows every little detail about His children: both the good and the bad. I know of no better way to recognize this than David's summation of God's awareness of our nature as revealed in Psalms 139. The inspired psalmist even said He knows when I sit down, when I rise, when I go out, and when I lie down. He can even perceive my thoughts from afar. The Lord even knows what we are about to say before we speak. David said God knows all of this because He made us.

Now, if God made us and knows all about us, He must care very deeply for His people, even when we make mistakes. We can see, then, why God's care and love will see us through the darkest hours. This very thought provokes deep thought and takes much of the sting out of our pain. Thus, if we want help when we experience suffering, we must ask for our Father's help like a child cries for his parents.

Since God made us capable of choices, we will experience pain for our wrong choices, but He can and will provide relief if we submit to His pattern of repentance and confession for our wrong choices. If God does not respond immediately, it is because His wisdom sees it is in our best interest to fully experience the situation, learn from it, and refuse to repeat the wrong we have done.

When David wrote his oft quoted twenty-third Psalm, he did not speak of avoiding the shadow of death, but he did say that the Shepherd would walk with him. This is evidence again of the Lord's interest in our deep trials and His readiness to bless and comfort us. Jeremiah expresses it like this, "It is of the Lord's mercies that we are not consumed because His compassion faileth not" (Lamentations 3:22).

We invite more pain if we reject the Father who made us or refuse His fellowship; we reduce our suffering immensely when we accept and invite His company.

An Unusual Journey from Pain to Happiness

The Lord knows life's experiences will often take us through valleys of anguish, pain, and misery. He also knows it is possible to turn these miserable experiences completely around and not just temporarily.

First, we often reach the erroneous conclusion that God does not want us to be happy. Such a feeling is the tool of our most bitter enemy, Satan. We do not enjoy the association with people who make us miserable. We naturally seek the company of those who make us feel good, who help us through bad times. If we believe God is against us, then we will avoid Him.

The Lord's advice and His will seem unusual at times. Note, for example, what has long been a recognized part of the Master Teacher's greatest sermon recorded in Matthew 5:1-12. One reason for this amazing message to His disciples was to help qualify them for their great work of encouraging and redeeming multitudes of people in distress or need. What seems unusual at first glimpse is the number of unpleasant or what some would call undesirable feelings or traits.

The King James Version of the Bible as well as some others use the word "blessed" to preface each of the beatitudes. Some other translations use the word "happy." If we examine the Webster's New Collegiate Dictionary, we find the definition of blessed: "A thing conducive to happiness or welfare." When we look at the definition of happy one meaning is "enjoying well being and contentment."

As we examine the blessings pronounced by Jesus, we note that quite often what we consider something bad or conducive to suffering, pain, and unhappiness, Jesus shows and promises the outcome will be happiness.

Verse 3 reads, "Blessed are the poor in spirit." To us that phrase may suggest poor self image. Jesus taught the good results of humility, though, to be the reward of taking part in the kingdom of heaven. Verse 4 says, "Blessed are they that mourn," which suggests sorrow, but Jesus promises comfort to those who mourn over things that are detrimental to us. "Blessed are the meek" is the expression in verse 5. Jesus is really promising happy results for those who realize they are not the most important being in the world. One who has true, proper respect for the Lord will not feel overly mighty and powerful in comparison to a perfect Redeemer.

The meek person has his/her emotions under control, and the result will produce happiness.

The blessing pronounced in Matthew 5:6 is "blessed are they which do hunger and thirst after righteousness, for they shall be filled." The very thought of hunger and thirst tends to produce pain. There is a beautiful song that compares the idea of a deer panting for water to the strong desire of one for spiritual food and drink. Such a proper desire for food for the soul will be rewarded and produce happiness for the hungry soul. Only those who have such a desire to meet the needs of the soul can be truly and eternally happy.

Verse 7 reads, "Blessed are the merciful, for they shall obtain mercy." Being merciful to others may require sacrifice and personal loss, but God's promise includes the mercy we all need. That valuable reward produces personal happiness beyond measure!

Verse 8 records a beautiful thought: "Blessed are the pure in heart, for they shall see God." When we find ourselves tempted to think evil thoughts that surely would invite misery, the idea of seeing God brings deliverance and a promise we all treasure.

When we are urged to disrupt harmony and add words and actions to prevent or destroy peace, we will do well to remember the blessing Jesus offers in verse 9: "Blessed are the peacemakers, for they shall be called the children of God." We have no choice in whom our earthly parents may be. Far more important is the fact that we choose whether or not we want to be a child of God. Peacemakers make that choice and benefit by becoming an heir of far more than the world can offer.

As we read verse 10, "Blessed are they which are persecuted," we may feel very distraught. When the Lord reveals the reason for this persecution, "for righteousness sake," the picture takes us back to happier feelings. And then as He reminds us of the end result, "for theirs is the kingdom of heaven," the reward overshadows the darkest moment. After all, heaven is what we all want above all other treasures. At first verse 11 does not seem pleasant at all: "Blessed are ye, when men shall revile you, and persecute you, and shall say all manner of evil against you falsely, for my sake." Still, when we consider all the Lord has done for us, the grateful individual should feel, "I'll do anything for my Lord with a positive attitude."

The conclusion of the beatitude section is a call to "rejoice and be exceeding glad, for great is your reward in heaven: for so persecuted they the prophets which were before you." Just to be placed in the company of the prophets in service is indeed marvelous, but to note that we can be with them in heaven is like a ray of sunshine on a gloomy, cloudy day.

From our reading of this section of the Gospel, we can see that the loving Savior can turn sorrow into joy if we allow Him to.

Turning Fear into Happiness

The remarkable twenty-third Psalm serves many wonderful purposes. It is used in funeral occasions so often we begin to attach that as the sole purpose to this masterpiece of David. It can actually fill a vacuum in our lives in many ways and comfort us in numerous situations.

Fear is indeed the father of much anguish and pain. It clothes itself in many styles. For example, we experience fear as wants, hunger, thirst, loneliness, and a need for protection and security; we can face the fear of rejection, mortality, and enemies. Sometimes we fear our physical or spiritual needs will not be met.

As remarkable as it may seem, David covers all these needs and fears in Psalm 23. Using the figure or illustration of a shepherd, he shows how these needs can be met and fears allayed. His first statement is the most inclusive, "The Lord is my shepherd." The words powerful and personal come to mind; the all-powerful, protective Lord is also a personal provider: "my shepherd." David states, "I shall not want" and immediately specifies a list of natural wants and shows how our perfect Shepherd meets these. "He maketh me to lie down in green pastures," suggesting the need for food and rest being amply supplied. "He leads me beside still waters" indicating plenty to satisfy thirst, but also still waters, not roaring, dangerous, fearful streams! When the soul is hurting (a spiritual need), He restores "my soul." Further protection and comfort are supplied: "He leads me in the paths of righteousness for His name's sake." Both the Lord and his beloved individual benefit.

The fear of the unknown, especially death, is a source of much concern for many. This did not hinder David. He says, "Yea though I walk through the valley of the shadow of death, I will fear no evil." The reason is mentioned: "For thou art with me." God is never so busy He cannot be with His child in death.

As he refers again to one of our greatest needs and fears (bodily sustenance), he states, "Thou preparest a table before me in the presence of my enemies." Even enemies of God and man will not prevent God's care. "Thou annointest my head with oil." Oil was used both to anoint (as a medicine) for bodily damage and for honoring one who was being placed in a high position. "My cup runneth over," suggesting an abundant supply to meet our needs. This could include the physical and spiritual needs, thus arresting other fears.

Security, assurance, and protection extending into eternity are provided in verse 6: "Surely goodness and mercy shall follow me all the days of my life, and I will dwell in the house of the Lord forever."

It seems there is little room for doubt about divine inspiration in this work of art. It is so refreshing and encouraging that David includes the solution to all our fears, doubts, and concerns in these six short verses.

If we are seeking answers to our miserable fears and their accompanying pain and agony, that answer is found when we accept the Lord as our shepherd. We are so much in need of One to guide us: "It is not in man that walketh to direct his own steps" (Jeremiah 10:23). We need One to bring us back from our sin: "All we like sheep have gone astray" (Isaiah 53:6). We need One who knows us well: "I am the good shepherd, and know my sheep, and am known of mine" (John 10:14). And we need One who take care of us when we fear: "Casting all your cares upon Him, for He careth for you" (I Peter 5:7). God provides all of these things and more.

Abused Fear and Worry

Dr. Murray Banks, in his book *What to Do until the Psychiatrist Comes,* expresses on page 25 an important view of worry: it is an emotional attitude accompanied with unpleasantness. He goes on to compare it to interest paid on trouble before it is due and further suggests it is a product of prolonged frustrations, doubts, conflicts, and chronic anxiety rooted in fear. It seems to me he has a handle on a great problem.

Worry does not necessarily destroy us; the way we react will destroy or develop us. Handled the proper way while making necessary adjustments, worry makes us better. Improper attention makes us worse. Fear is a cause and fuel for worry. To allow all thinking to turn to fear and worry will destroy us. It is a habit that must be changed. When changed, it makes one stronger. To fail to adjust and to ignore proper control will allow fear and worry to grow like a mushroom. The results will produce loss of control or gain of control depending on what we do about our worry.

We must decide what is truly most important to us, do all we can to remove every obstacle that stands in the way, and replace the worry with good thoughts or materials.

If we need help to resolve our fears and worry, we must seek it. If it is totally beyond our control, we must direct our attention on some really valuable work or calling. One way or another, we must do something to address worry, though. If we try to ignore or cover it, it will grow into a giant or crop up somewhere else or in another form.

Never forget God is always there to help His people, and some of His followers will also be available. We never have to be alone.

Perhaps more of us should move attention to the One who created us than to the fears and worry we created ourselves.

Man's Introduction to Fear

Did you ever stop to think that the first experience with fear was when Adam and Eve separated themselves from God by their sin? They had never known this pain as long as they respected and obeyed the Father, nor could they find relief and comfort away from God. Even when they suffered punishment as a consequence for their sin, they could not find relief until they returned to their Maker.

Much of our pain and sorrow is visited upon us for exactly the same cause. God alone has all the answers; He provides help and relief through His guide book and His ministry servants. If and when our helpers use God's directions, our deepest pain can be released and eased.

Both God and man are social beings. When we meet God, one of the most beautiful experiences begins, and it continues as long as we seek, meet, and stay with our Father.

Fear as a Blessing

Why did God give us the ability to fear? We have seen that it can be a friend, when it brings us closer to our faith in our Father. Fear also has a protective purpose, which God knew when he endowed us with the ability to fear. There are good qualities to this natural part of our being.

Let us note some very positive qualities of this emotion. If we approach it in this light, we will recognize it as a friend. It helps keep us from getting too close to the edge of a cliff or precipice, from getting in the water when we cannot swim or when conditions are hazardous even for good swimmers. It may prevent us from lying or repeating gossip because we do not wish to invite the unpleasant results of sorrow, guilt, or loss of acceptance. Fear can discourage us from going to dangerous places, associating with bad people, contracting disease, or causing injuries to our bodies. It is actually a necessary part of our lives. Perhaps one of the very best parts of God's revelation to us is the necessity to fear God and give glory to Him (Revelation 14:7).

If we permit it, God has given us the ability to control fear and to allow it to serve its intended purpose. It is a guardian for both our physical and spiritual well-being. It may be that fear is actually one of God's greatest blessings. Proper fear can bring about an essential change and will actually prevent a more miserable type of fear. A second of fear can prevent an act or move that could produce a long-lasting, negative fear. It may change our lives in a positive way. This is obvious in the stories of many Bible characters. No doubt you can recall someone whose life was improved because of the prompting of fear reminding them of the consequences of unchanged attitudes or acts. Fear of both current and eternal results often produces changes in lifestyles.

Fear of both current and eternal results often produces changes in lifestyles.

The cause for our fears should be carefully examined to determine if it is a genuine or imagined concern, or if it is a friend or a foe, a blessing or a curse, produced by God's wisdom or our self-induced practices.

A Great Need for Humanity

Perhaps the greatest need for humanity is spiritual security. We cannot be free of fear without our Lord's help. Let us examine another area of fear and its real solution.

Spiritual darkness hovers over our entire world. The only power to overcome this dread is found in God. David found the source of help in the past only in God's protection. Present relief is found in the same source.

Exodus 14:15 provides an interesting illustration of our premise. Moses and the children of Israel felt a natural fear at the Red Sea. The Lord asked, "Why do you cry to me?" When they decided to trust God, they accepted His means of escape from their enemies and used a sea of threat as an avenue of escape.

The application for us is in asking how we can overcome fear and proceed toward our goals. Trust in God is our answer as well. It will motivate us to be filled with a desire to please Him and accept His help. If God had the power to make our world, including mankind, He can deliver His creation from harm. Does He not have the right to ask us to meet His conditions? When we trust Him to the degree that we accept and apply His conditions, we prove our faith and step out on His promises. Like the Israelites, why do we cry to God for relief and refuse to accept it, adding fear to our other miseries?

Our greatest cause of fear is a lack of trust and faith in our spiritual Savior. Doubt is a parent of fear!

A New Testament example of our solution to fear is recorded in Matthew 8. The cause of this fear was not really the raging sea, but a lack of real faith in Jesus. Our Lord took advantage of the situation to first rebuke those afraid, then to prove that He was worthy of their faith and the solution to their fear. Verse 26 records, "And He saith unto them, why are ye fearful, oh ye of little faith? Then He arose and rebuked the winds and the sea, and there was a great calm."

Doubt is a parent of fear!

We may face dangers that require a greater faith than raging waters. Jesus may employ different methods or means today, but His power is still unlimited for those whose faith and trust grasp His promise by meeting His conditions.

Matthew 6:30 calls attention to another faith-building example. He reminds those who lacked the proper faith that if He takes care of things that soon perish, surely He will save the souls of those who obey Him. Right priorities remind us that all material things perish, but we have an eternal soul. Mark 8:36-37 reminds us that it is worth any price or sacrifice of material things to save our souls. He asks, "What shall a man give in exchange for his soul?"

The interesting fact is those who take care of the soul will follow God's plan for taking care of less important things. God's saving grace is channeled through His love. Our love for Him enables us to trust His conditions and plans and embrace His blessings by proving our faith and trust through our proper response and acceptance.

Obedient faith turns failure into success and triumph; it alleviates unnecessary fear.

Suffering or Blessings Are Often Produced at Home

The homes we grow up in all produce a great measure of the pain or genuine pleasure we all experience. In turn, the homes we build will determine a huge degree of misery or happiness for those we love.

God's plan for the home, from the beginning, was for it to be a place of love and nurturing. Second to love of our Father, the love for one's mate was to be at the top of our priority list. When that home is blessed with children, the Lord planned for them to enjoy a loving, nurturing environment. Part of this growth and development is to be the exposure to parents who dearly love and respect one another. The results of such a relationship will insure devotion and faithfulness to the spouse for as long as both live. Every child deserves and needs that comfort and immeasurable blessing. The family unit with this atmosphere will include the Lord and produce the strongest defenses against the world and all enemies. True, even the most perfect home will experience some pain, disappointment, and heartache, but the amount can be reduced considerably in a home surrounded by faith and love.

Our children need to know about our heavenly Father. The place our Creator and Redeemer holds in the heart is often determined by the homes we grow up in. Children will develop love and trust for God, better face difficulty, and set proper priorities when properly taught by the word and example of their home. This example will give them the best ally to defend them in a cruel world. Children will have great difficulty understanding the true love of a heavenly Father, Director, and Defender if they have not experienced it in the type of home God planned.

Lola and I experienced the sad side of this situation in one place where we served as missionaries for several years. She taught a class of teen-aged girls. The task and privilege was made more difficult because she could not appropriate some of the best illustrations in her class. For example, one older student said, "No one ever told me they loved me." When Lola responded, "I love you," the girl was embarrassed. She could not understand a heavenly Father's love because she had not truly experienced an earthly father's, mother's, or family's love. Those who have experienced a similar situation will possess a much deeper appreciation for the home as God would have it.

We all develop attitudes about people and the Lord at home. If we do not get to build the proper foundation, pain and suffering will be multiplied as we face relationships, authority, and proper conduct habits for years to come. When confronted with these necessary experiences, where can one go for help and guidance?

God wants to be our guide and helper! The sooner we learn and accept that, our problems will grow smaller and our resources for solutions will become greater.

The author and his wife on their 50th wedding anniversary, surrounded by their children and grandchildren.

Some Things to Learn and Be Encouraged By

Recently I noticed a scripture that I had not really examined before. Two things of great importance come to mind. One is, if I conduct myself in the wrong way then God will allow me to suffer. The other is, if evil people abuse me then they must answer to the greatest Judge and the One who holds our eternal reward in His hands. Note both of these standards in Malachi 3:5—"And I will come near to you in judgment, and I will be a swift witness against the sorcerer and against the adulteress and against false swearers, and against those that oppress the hireling in his wages, the widow and the fatherless, and turn aside the stranger from his right, and fear me not, saith the Lord of hosts." Verse 6 affirms that this God is always and forever dependable: "For I am the Lord; I change not."

All that is involved and all those with the characteristics involved are as accountable to God today as when the inspired writer first penned those words. Our loving Father still protects his own and punishes those who hurt his children.

When we read the last book of the Old Testament and are ready to begin the New Testament, we are impressed with the past and present, marvelous plan of our loving Father. The conclusion points to three basic parts of a perfect plan: faith, grace, and obedience. As I look at that summation, I recall once being called a legalist when I spoke at a college in Kentucky because I emphasized the need for obedience to God's laws. I realize I could have spoken at length about grace and faith with that professor's blessing; however, when I included the means by which we attain grace by obedient faith, he could not appreciate that logical, true conclusion.

Faith without obedience to the Master's plan is not real, true faith

Think about it: God's great gift cannot be produced by man or bought by man yet is often rejected by man. The greater part of pain, misery, disappointment, and evil is a result of not embracing God's grace by His prescribed method—obedient faith. Faith in the absence of obedience to the Master's plan is not real, true faith. If I truly believe that God is who He claims to be, I will not be happy until I have pleased Him by doing whatever He asks.

Most of us can still remember the sweet, comforting feeling that came from knowing we had pleased our loving parents. Our heavenly Father will be pleased and reward us when we obey. We will make Him miserable when we disobey. Which choice do we make? Obey His will, and produce a double happiness, or refuse and leave God and ourselves unhappy.

Growth and Service through Suffering

We have noted before that there are reasons, good ones, for some unpleasant experiences in our lives. Sometimes we are able to grow and serve others because of our pain. Have you ever considered the treasure that resulted from the suffering of Joseph? There was jealousy and abuse from his own brothers, separation from his family, slavery in a distant land.

Things got worse still when he was imprisoned because of a false accusation of an evil, lustful woman. The very depth of his misery in prison placed him in position to render his greatest service. He was a model prisoner and impressed the keeper. He helped his fellow prisoners. One of the prisoners Joseph helped regain freedom forgot about this help and failed to speak well to the king, which could have improved Joseph's state (Genesis 39-40). Chapter 41 informs us that two years later Pharaoh had a most disturbing dream that none of his counselors could interpret. At that point the former ungrateful fellow prisoner remembered Joseph and informed his master of Joseph's special character and ability. The result was that Pharaoh called on Joseph to interpret the troublesome dream, a task that brought the reward of freedom as well as a high position of power and trust, second in command to Pharaoh himself.

Still later, Joseph's hard-earned position made it possible to care for his family in time of famine and misery. This included his father and his jealous brothers, who had sold him into slavery and caused him much pain. When those guilty, nervous brothers learned who their benefactor was, they were fearfully concerned. Joseph confronted them with a remarkable statement recorded in Genesis 45:5, "Now therefore be not grieved nor angry with yourselves, that ye sold me hither, for God did send me before you to preserve life." In verse 7 he states that God sent him to "preserve you a posterity and to save your lives." That is exactly what happened! God allowed Joseph's suffering to turn into an opportunity for him to help his people.

Consider these following valuable lessons drawn from this series of painful experiences in the life of Joseph:

1. The darkest hour does indeed often come before dawn.

2. Those are rewarded who never give up on our heavenly Father.

3. The Lord never forgets His own no matter where we are. It never gets too dark for God to see us (Psalms 139:12).

4. No matter where we find ourselves, there are opportunities to do good and serve Him.

5. Despite what happens, we must never forget God and that He loves the faithful.

6. Often, the worse things get, the better the results of the final outcomes.

7. Our worst ordeals may prove to be the best time to exert our godly influence.

8. No matter who else may forget us, God never does.

9. Like Joseph, we must never lose sight of the end result and rewards for our faithful service.

10. No matter how deep the pain of life's experiences get, the experience of eternity

away from God and His family would be far worse.

11. Nothing really valuable ever comes without cost.

12. God's gifts will outweigh and outlast the most valuable earthly, fleeting treasure!

13. We must never sell out to the devil. He can offer temporary pleasures and, in the end, eternal pain. He has nothing good and eternal to offer.

14. Joseph suffered at the hands of those who should have loved and protected him, but gained what they never could have given him.

15. Our hero never seemed to blame God or anyone else for all his suffering. Ask yourself the question: who, casting blame, has ever relieved or resolved pain?

16. Because of his prison experience and its outcome, Joseph gained influence over an area far beyond Egypt.

17. The total of experiences we receive can fuel a light that brightens an unbelievably vast area.

No matter who sits in the throne of power or highest position in any country, God still sits on the throne of heaven. We will only be here a short while, but those who serve the King of Kings can reign with Him eternally. No power on earth can prevent God's plan and power from serving its purpose!

For example, God drew the line on Haman's plan and the king's edict to destroy all the Jews under his influence in the book of Esther. Had evil man's will been carried out, the seed of Abraham would not have existed through which our Savior came.

Even the death of Jesus Christ and the gates of hell could not prevent Christ from building His church (Matthew 16:18, Acts 2:38-47).

Even Satan cannot take us where we do not agree to go, and when we are saved by God's plan, only our life choices can keep us from heaven. We make the decision to obey or reject the Lord, and we decide to stay with or leave God. The influence of one or two good individuals can affect people far and wide, such as Mordecai and Esther (Esther 8:17). Those who truly believe in and trust God will find a way in His word to serve and save others from more pain and suffering and be a positive influence on a host of others.

A Simple Way to Overcome Temptation

Most of us would agree that one of the greatest sources of pain and suffering is temptation. The big question that looms in the heart of all good people is *how do I deal with temptation?* The first and best answer to this mammoth question is found in the example of Jesus Christ.

When Satan took Him at His most vulnerable time to tempt Him, he exhausted his resources with his three best attempts. Jesus resisted every effort with three simple words: "It is written" (Matthew 4:1-11).

Remember Jesus was in human form, and He was hungry after a forty-day fast. Many other references are made to His being hungry, tired, discouraged, denied, betrayed, and abused in so many ways, yet He never lost sight of His purpose and the end results of His heavenly home. He had given up home to complete a plan for us to go to heaven. His work was completed when He faithfully carried out His Father's will and that included overcoming the devil.

We have the assurance that God will never ever tempt any person (James 1:13). Suffice it to conclude that it is never right to blame God when we are tempted. When our enemy, Satan, tempts us, it is comforting to know that when we use the tried and successful plan Jesus used in the desert, we too can overcome the devil's best efforts. It follows then that the more familiar we are with what God says, the better equipped we are to prevent being overcome by temptation and its results of intense pain.

A Case for Pain as a Friend

Heaven seems much more inviting because of suffering pain and other kindred unpleasant experiences. If all the beauty and joy was never interrupted and marred by some misery, we might not be interested in leaving this world for a better state. There are so many things that attract us here, our thoughts of heaven might be few.

The very thoughts of and desires for heaven actually prevent much pain because they invite us to prepare for it instead of giving in to temptation. Matthew 6:20-21 says, "Lay up for yourselves in heaven…for where your treasure is there will your heart be also."

Suffering can make us better. For one thing, through suffering we are prepared to sympathize with, comfort, and aid others. It also equips others to comfort us when we experience burdens. This earthly comfort can have heavenly rewards as we please our Father through such service.

Remember Jesus' greatest victory was achieved when His cruel enemies tried to cause His permanent death. Even on the cross He prayed for His enemies. Think how they must have felt when they learned He had risen from the dead. His victory over death, hell, and the grave made possible the victory of every one of us who embraces His soul-saving plan. As terrible as His pain was, He no doubt realized He was better off than those who placed Him there. Our pain may turn our losses into victory too!

Through suffering we are prepared to sympathize with, comfort, and aid others.

We are likely to appreciate the privilege and power of prayer when we are made to feel the need of a power beyond man's ability. I know the older I get the more I find the need to appreciate the blessings of prayer and the hope of heaven. A deeper beauty and stronger spirit have become evident in the lives of some dear, beloved, suffering Christians.

The beauty and strength derived from Romans 8:28, "All things work together for good to them that love God, to them who are called according to His purpose," is much more lovely and apparent after we have endured and survived some bitter experience and witnessed the benefits derived.

Only truth learned and applied as we travel the journey of this life can prepare us for heaven, and both pleasant and unpleasant circumstances are vital teachers. Very often we cannot see the value of a matter or circumstance until we have experienced both the beginning and the end.

We can be best prepared to cope with both good and bad experiences when we are forewarned that both will be a part of our life. I am so grateful our loving Father revealed the fact that among the pleasant and good would also be pain and evil. No doubt this state of things accounts for the statement of Jesus recorded in Matthew 16:24, "If any man will come after me, let him deny himself and take up his cross and follow me." Note also I Timothy 3:12 says, "All that will live godly in Christ Jesus shall suffer persecution." Yes, even the best of us will suffer some. Would we prefer some suffering now as a result of walking with the Lord here or be on the other side and suffer eternally? Hopefully some of the things we have called attention to will help us see why and realize that good comes to us who never forget where our hope and help lie.

Coping with the How and Why of Life

Logic and experience reveal to the truly honest person that one must not become overly concerned with the why of life's ways. Knowing how to deal with life as it is must not be clouded with the question why. The sooner we understand that God's power and love are unlimited, the sooner we embrace Him. When we accept the nature of our Creator despite the fact that we cannot always understand why our Lord is like He is, the less important the why becomes. At that point we come to recognize how to adapt His plan and accept and apply His way. No one must ever presume to be smarter than God! To simply recognize that His way is the best way will break down barriers and allow us to accept His solution to any problem.

I can never know someone I never talk to, listen to, or spend some time with. Like Abraham, we need to become a friend to God. Friendship is a two-way street.

The Lord is ready; are we ready to accept Him as both friend and authority? We are assured that the way we approach any situation can overshadow the questioning of why the problem exists, making the question less important.

We are all naturally surrounded by people who are inconsistent. One of the great traits of our heavenly Father is consistency. Because His laws are always consistent, if we break a law and experience unpleasant results, we can also expect to receive reward when we conform to His plan. If both these principles are not true, God would not be dependable, and everything would be mass confusion. The effect of this chaos would bring far more problems, pain, and suffering than we have ever experienced. The wages of sin is death, but the gift of God is eternal (Romans 6:23). This is the bottom line at the end of our life. The best prevention for and solution to our difficulties is to simply accept God's way and not be too concerned with why. God has all the answers if we allow Him to govern our life.

Fire blesses, hinders, or destroys depending on how we respect and use it. We all understand that concept and do not ask why. In the same way, our choice to follow or ignore God's laws can bless, hinder, or destroy us. If good or bad results did not follow actions, life would be miserable, and it would make no difference how we lived. How confusing life would be if we never knew what results our actions would provide!

❖ ❖ ❖

We are made in the image of God. Since that is a desirable fact, we should try to be as much like our Father as possible. Children begin very early to imitate the parent. God-fearing parents set the proper example first, then require respect and obedience. If we were blessed with godly parents, we learned at an early age that rewards or punishments followed our actions. We also see the results of those who did not respect home and their parents.

> We should try to be as much like our Father as possible.

Consistency is rewarded at every level in life! The more like Father we become, the better we understand Him; the more we appreciate His ways and the sooner we apply and require them, the more our sorrows and disappointments will lessen.

A child may not understand why the parent always punishes his disrespect and disobedience; however, the more mature we become the better we understand why. The lesson becomes very clear when we have children of our own. We then recognize that love demands accountability in the interest of wellbeing and safety.

Mature spiritual adults find it easier to better understand the wisdom of God. Wise Solomon expresses it like this, "My son, despise not the chastening of the Lord; neither be weary of His correction, for whom the Lord loveth He correcteth, even as a father the son in whom he delighteth" (Proverbs 3:11-12). God says, "As many as I love I rebuke and chasten" (Revelation 3:19). Both the Old and the New Testaments abound with the words and acts of the Father attending to this fundamental truth.

Next time we feel the need to ask why, we should rather remind ourselves of the Father who loves us enough to provide heaven, if we only believe and obey.

Wise Planning for the Future

In God's plan we do not find it necessary to just wait and see what the future may bring. His love and consistency properly applied enable us to see ahead and prepare for the future. His gift of choice enables us to make choices that produce desired results. It is true that the road of life will present its hills and valleys, but after all, the end result is the most important goal of our lives! We can take encouragement from Romans 8:31—"If God be for us, who can be against us?" Foes will be encountered, but the victory belongs to God. As surely as that is true, His faithful followers will share in that victory.

The wise, perceptive individual will keep this idea in mind: I must include God in all of my plans to insure a happier future and less pain.

I once wrote a song that contains the lines "I always knew that I'd walk down this road some day, but I did not know yesterday that it would be today." No doubt many have experienced the same results and feeling. At the same time, we do know that much of the future depends on what we do today, just as today was determined in large measure by what choices we made yesterday. If we therefore exercise discretion and wisdom in making good decisions today, there is a far better chance that tomorrow will be better.

Today's friends and associates will be a major determining factor in our future. Proper selection of friends helps to determine when and where the road will end. We must choose our associates wisely! The wrong kind of company will make the journey more difficult. It is equally true that good friends are always there to lend a hand, lift a burden, encourage us, and make the bumps smoother. Galatians 6:2 reveals that Christians bear one another's burdens; however, "evil communications corrupt good manners" (I Corinthians 15:33).

Much of the future depends on what we do today.

Wise people know that Jesus is a trusted friend. Other friends should be selected on the basis of who will select the ultimate best friend, Jesus. Those who reject Him will have an adverse effect on our entire future!

Whatever pain we may be called upon to endure, our Savior and Friend has already experienced and overcome. He understands our trials, and if we walk with Him we will go where He is. Faith in that very fact will serve us when we feel ready to give up, but it will also reduce the number and degree of our pains. "There hath no temptation taken you but such as is common to man; but God is faithful who will not suffer you to be tempted above that ye are able, but will with the temptation make a way to escape that you may be able to bear it" (I Corinthians 10:13).

Afraid to Face Pain?

Many who will not enjoy or experience some of the most beautiful and pleasant blessings of life have denied themselves of these. Why? Because they were afraid to venture out into the world because pain and evil are out there. Remember that the turtle cannot see, know, or even move until he sticks his head and feet out of his shell. He may move slowly, but he does move and experience life. Actually, he risks as much danger at times inside his shell as he does out. If he is in the wrong place, a vehicle can crush him whether he is inside or out of his protective covering.

When I reach the end of life's journey, I know I will have seen and experienced some bad, painful circumstances; however, I want to see and experience the beauty and good God has created for me to enjoy. Go with God and good friends who appreciate Him and His creation. Otherwise, the entire journey will be a miserable disappointment. Even if we embark on the road less traveled, if we invite the Lord to be with us, we will both reach the prize of heaven at the end of the trip.

Can We Live with Criticism?

Why should I try to accomplish something knowing that I risk being hurt by rejection and judgment? Remember the biggest mistake we could make is to do nothing. We may miss some unpleasant situations, but be certain we will also deny ourselves of the joy and satisfaction of a good deed well done, the reward of victory, or the applause of good people. These will far outweigh the criticism of the miserable people who sit in judgment for their pleasures. Far beyond that God made me, and, rightfully so, He requires something of me. Also, His rewards are the best, and they last forever.

Criticism always hurts, and it may be more painful if it is unjust. We must remember that our Lord was often criticized, and it was never deserved. He accepted it to help us, and we have learned many lessons as a benefit of His pain. When His followers do right, we may be criticized; however, when we are beat down for doing good, the Lord still approves our actions. His judgment is the most important in our lives. If all men approved us, we would find ourselves on the opposite side of our Redeemer. What hope could we expect then? James 4:4 informs us that a friend of the world is an enemy of God. Our life choices may decide our friends and enemies at the same time. Who has more to offer us? Where would the ultimate greater pain be? Note the words of the inspired penman in James 1:10, "Do I seek to please men? For if I yet pleased man, I should not be the servant of Christ." We should remember this Biblical principle when we fear or grow weary of criticism.

Also, we should take into account that condemnation provides an opportunity to develop self control. Through patience and comfort of the scriptures, we can have hope (Romans 4:4).

Examination of Criticism:

What can we gain? Examine this factor carefully and prayerfully. If we find the least amount of merit in the criticism we must learn from it, make adjustments, and make it work for us and not against us.

If it is totally unjust criticism, consider the source. Does it come from the type of person that always finds fault with everything and everyone? Does it flow from a heart that is simply opposed to my moral standard or efforts to do good and please God? Would I really want the approval of the one who tries to tear me down? Does the criticism affirm my views and standards of living? Could I please my Lord *and* the one who criticizes me at the same time?

When I weigh all the evidence and answer all these questions I can make changes from positive criticism or realize that the one tearing me down is in opposition to the Lord my actions please; both of these actions can actually turn sorrow into joy.

Coping with Pain

Is there a source of comfort that generally eases any pain I may be called upon to endure?

Let us first assure ourselves of the fact that we can never blame God when we are tempted, hurt, or face a loss.

It is never in order to begin with such false assumptions such as saying, "What did I do to deserve this bitter situation? It must be all my fault." At times the problem is a result of a personal error, but not always. Look for other causes.

A better approach is simply, if I can successfully resolve this and know it is not a result of personal failure, I have removed part of the sting and guilt and produced some relief.

If I conclude it was the result of a foolish mistake that I really know I should not have made, I must assume the responsibility. In such cases I at least know where to begin to correct my habits or failures. At that point I can take satisfaction in learning a lesson. Also, I can feel safer and more comfortable in the future. I should now grow stronger or more mature. Knowing the real results of following a certain path will enable me to choose a different, better one. Now I have God's help and new-found knowledge. Therefore my pain was not totally in vain!

Did my suffering or uncomfortable situation result from my association with the wrong type of friends? Again, if it becomes obvious this is the source, I have gained another source of prevention. I can seek stronger friends who help rather than hinder my choices and actions.

If I conclude I have offended my well-being by going to a place that produced or had some part in my misery I can choose not to frequent that place again. My education has improved.

I should determine to learn something from every unpleasant experience. We can turn most losses into gain.

Did my personal choice or mistake bring discomfort or embarrassment to another? If so, my next move should be to apologize to the offended party and seek forgiveness. In so doing we show the victim that we are big enough to face up to responsibility. We may strengthen a friendship and gain more self esteem. We will also become a better friend and learn not to repeat actions that hinder friendships. I can make better decisions and exercise more self control. I have done what I would hope another would do for me.

This simple approach to every unpleasant experience is another refreshing method of turning a foe into a friend.

More Lessons at the Feet of an Unexpected Teacher

I have been blessed all my life by benefiting from very special teachers; however, some of my most valuable lessons were learned from unusual teachers or unexpected situations. Solomon uses an interesting statement in Proverbs 27:17, "As iron sharpens iron, so one man sharpens another." This is an unusual comparison, but true in both cases. Quite often improvement is produced by what appears to be painful or destructive. We may determine if the result is good or bad. We may not always understand how God can accomplish some of the best results in our lives.

The wise person learns from the effects of every experience. As we examine the first part of Solomon's reasoning, "iron sharpens iron," we can easily apply this idea. Garden or kitchen tools grow dull with use. Other tools can be used that are abrasive to improve the cutting edge of those tools. What seems to wear away a part of the implement or tool actually sharpens and returns it to a useful state.

God gives us opportunities for self improvement, but He also provides others to make us better or more qualified for a task, duty, responsibility, position, or profession.

If those who train and develop us never challenge, correct, or make us pliable and responsible, they cannot possibly prepare us for the upcoming tasks of life. Sometimes the instructions, assignments, projects, etc. may seem too difficult; we may see no reason or connection between the goal and the method of getting there. We may feel exhausted, imposed upon, disgusted, angry, and mistreated during the training process.

At the end of the experience, we may feel we have earned a worthwhile goal and be grateful to the person or persons who seemed insensitive and abusive. We can now see some sense in the process and method. Knowing what was done was all in our best interest, we can have that great feeling of confidence and be ready to begin a desired chapter in our life. It was worth it all because we can finally do what we planned and dreamed of doing.

You may remember me referencing an article I wrote entitled "All I Ever Needed to Know I Learned in The Cotton Patch." Hand picking and chopping cotton are two of the hardest, most back-breaking jobs we could do; however, I learned some things there that have proved to be my most valuable assets, things that can be applied to any task, job, or position I ever attained.

It is true, it is a proven fact: our greatest treasures may not always be the polished professor in the class room of the most highly acclaimed educational facility. Sometimes it is a seemingly menial task that becomes the greatest lesson for success: bringing satisfaction in learning, teaching us to accept authority and do the best job we can, and inspiring us to apply ourselves in any learning situation.

We are blessed indeed when we have been educated, sharpened, and polished in the classroom of hard knocks as well as the proven classrooms of well-rounded educational universities, the schools that develop the physical, mental, and spiritual parts of our well being.

The true learning experience is never all about self. Only when we are taught to help others and honor the Giver of every blessing (our Creator and God) have we earned a degree in the highest halls of honor.

Our God expects us to do the best we can with what we have! He can use the total personal experience, both good and bad, enjoyable and painful, to prepare us for the best here and eternally.

Teach Me — Try Me — Test Me

One is not always an enemy who tries my patience or tests my character. None of us arrived at a current acceptable status without good teachers, and sometimes the best education comes from situations that bring patience and strengthen character. It is regrettable that some become angry or disturbed when others do not accept them or when others try to correct some foolish, dangerous attitudes or lifestyles. What could be a perfect opportunity to grow only brings unhappiness to all in such situations.

I am thankful that doctors, friends, and family have been interested enough in me to correct or advise me, helping me make changes or adjustments even though it hurt at the time. I would never have been successful or perhaps alive had it not been for others informing me of errors and helping me make necessary adjustments even to the current time.

Many years ago I learned that metal not properly tempered (a process usually done by fire), will not serve its purpose. Iron can become so hard it cannot be filed, ground, or sharpened to meet some need. Iron improperly prepared may become so brittle it is of no use.

I continue to learn that people who have not been tempered by trials and some unpleasant experiences are of little use to others. They may be unable to understand people or to sympathize when it is needed.

The inspired James wrote about the trying of faith and how it results in patience that helps perfect us and our work (James 1:2-4). I know of no truly successful individual who has not been able to exercise a good measure of patience. That came in part by some trials along the way.

"The trials of your faith, being much more precious than of gold that perishes, though it be tried by fire, might be found unto praise and honor and glory at the appearing of Jesus Christ" (I Peter 1:7). Gold is recognized as one of the most valuable treasures in the world. The process that makes it so precious includes purification by fire. The trials of life may help increase our value and usefulness. The recognition of this fact helps us use some of our pain and suffering for good rather than allowing it to hinder us or become so discouraged that we want to withdraw in depression or give up on life.

My own earthly parents loved me so much that they guided me, taught me, advised me, and made me accountable to them and to others—especially to God. What they required was not always pleasant at the time. As I matured I recognized true love and desire for what was in my best interest was involved in their guidance. My heavenly Father also directs and corrects me while requiring me to be accountable to Him and others. At times that has not been pleasant; in fact it has been painful, sacrificial at times, but I have come to fully realize that He never requires anything that is not best for me in the end.

When I determine to make even unpleasant, hurtful experiences inflicted by others become acceptable by applying them to my growth and development, I become a better person. Through more recent years, I have undergone several surgeries. They were extremely painful at times, always inconvenient as they interrupted my well-intended plans. However, I fully realize that without these I would have suffered much more pain. Also, I can now encourage others as a result of these interruptions and unpleasant life experiences.

Learning that the suffering of life can teach us lessons will help us mature into people who can truly help others and thereby appear more like our suffering Savior, Christ Jesus!

Motivator or Destroyer

It can be healthy to remember that what motivates one may destroy another. We each make the decision as to which direction we turn, and God and godly friends will help us if we choose the right one. One person may make a negative comment about us; human nature is such that we will suffer agonizing pain each time this occurs. However, there are many others ready to help us overcome, and the Lord is always available and capable of assisting us.

Shall we choose to use all the available help to prove the offending party wrong? Shall we just give in to the one who has hurt us? Will we decide to conduct our life so that it becomes obvious someone has erred against us, either on purpose or because of misinformation? Furthermore, did this person really intend to harm us?

The decisions we make will add to the insult or prove we are the kind of strong person who seeks to do right under any circumstance. As surely as we make the correct choice we will become a stronger, happier person with an improved reputation.

Guilt: Friend or Foe?

Even guilt can be a friend and tool to motivate and encourage one to correct the cause. Since God endowed us with the quality to feel guilt, it is obvious our loving Creator designed it to help us, not hinder us. Guilt prompts a re-examining of our belief and behavior. If it causes us to make necessary changes, it has served a God-given purpose. If not, we will continue to be engulfed in misery, and it is obvious we have prevented this trait from serving its proper function.

I really appreciate what Dr. Bill Flatt says about guilt: "All guilt is not bad. Redemptive guilt is like a fire alarm that signals when something is wrong. The wise person is alerted to the alarm and tries to take care of the problem" (Flatt 34).

Guilt gives us an opportunity to repent, correct the wrong, and get back to living a normal, even better life.

It also serves as a reminder not to place ourselves in the dreaded situation again.

Think how guilty King David felt when his series of sins resulted in adultery, murder, cheating, and using his position to excuse himself while taking advantage of his situation. Later that burden of guilt became so heavy he found solace only in unloading it by confessing to God, repenting, and asking God's forgiveness (II Samuel 12; Psalms 32).

May we determine to use guilt for the purpose God gave it—allowing it to motivate us to correct the wrong and remind us in the future not to ignore our conscience and sound reasoning.

Let us remember that guilt is designed to stimulate us to provoke thought, seek recourse, find a way to remove the pain, and determine to refuse to repeat actions that caused that pain.

One pound of guilt can prevent a ton of future misery. A few hours can protect our life time and our eternity with our Father!

If we were blessed by good parents, we were conditioned to feel guilty when it is appropriate. As surely as we learn the principles of the followers of the Lord, we will sense guilt when we reject right and embrace wrong.

Many of us are wise and choose our friends with great care. We do well to exercise extreme caution in our choice of the use or rejection of our attributes and habits.

Obviously guilt produces misery and hurt; however, it can be a blessing—we decide if it is a friend or enemy.

Preparation for Reducing Pain and Increasing Happiness

The following might also be considered as remedies for souls in pain:

- Blessed is that one who has tasted the tears from his own eyes for he shall better understand the tears of others.

- One can only truly appreciate the heights of success who has experienced the depths of failure.

- Only they who have felt the misery of illness can really appreciate good health.

- Acquaintance with sorrow prepares us to fully enjoy happiness when it does enter our life.

- The strongest man is the one who hurts when he sees another in the throes of pain and sorrow.

- Will you be prepared when success is ready for you? Only if you have won many battles over failure.

- The eye of the beholder is trained by both beautiful and ugly scenes in life.

- Not a few who think they have reached the winner's circle are disappointed to learn they really lost. On the other hand, many who felt they were losers learned they had really reached the most important goal of life.

- Those who labor hardest to succeed are the same ones who truly enjoy and appreciate success.

- The highest wall is not necessarily the strongest. Much depends on that portion which cannot be seen.

- Beauty cannot be measured by only what one sees on the outside. The inside is where the beauty, or lack of it, is found.

- The best friend is the one who not only knows our achievements and talents, but one who knows our failures and weaknesses and remains a friend still.

- We may miss a friend most when he or she is gone. This experience should inspire us to appreciate those who are still with us.

- When we call on a friend we bless two people.

- We can only enjoy food to the greatest degree when we have experienced hunger.

- The greatest inspiration is found in our everyday experiences. Be certain you make note of many of them.

- We may easily forget some people, but must make sure we develop such strong relationships with those who are good examples and influences that we never forget them. If we fail to do so, we pay the price of losing many beautiful memories.

- Some quit when they are ahead; others simply reach higher!

- We know the real difference in up and down only when we have experienced both.

- To some life is a bowl of cherries. To others life is a bowl of pits. To a large measure, we each determine which it is. The wise are grateful for this personal responsibility!

- God lets us decide how we live our lives, but no really happy person leaves God out of his or her plans.

- Dreams that do not include the Lord will always turn out to be nightmares.

- Nightmares brought on by irresponsibility leave heavy tracks on our hearts.

- Never forget that it takes all four seasons to make a year; it also takes body, mind, soul, and spirit to make a complete person.

- Obviously the best teachers are those who teach the truth. Wise people choose those teachers and benefit the most.

- One who rides a wild horse must be prepared both to be thrown and to make a rough landing.

- Wisdom always blesses those who entertain it with respect.

- God's richest blessings are always wasted when we do not return a good portion to Him.

- Humility will raise me higher than boasting, haughtiness, and self righteousness combined.

- The most eloquent speaker who is ashamed or afraid to include God in his or her speeches is in reality a poor speaker.

- Those who are ashamed to own God cannot own any of the most precious possessions now or eternally.

- Those who never count their blessings are poor indeed no matter what they own!

- Consideration of others will beget attention.

- Love not only makes the world go round, but also makes it revolve more harmoniously.

- God did not only put the twinkle in the stars, but He also put the stars in the sky.

- Distance alone does not determine the measure of the walk, nor does time alone determine the value of our labor.

- All who walk in a parade do not accomplish a valuable purpose.

- It is not the beginning of the task but rather the end that determines the results and value.

- The smallest beginning accomplished with determined effort can produce good and long-lasting effects.

- He who works to prepare for the night will also see good results during the day.

- It is a blessed fact that all predictions do not come to pass.

- The sun shines brightest for those who recognize its Creator.

- We may not be able to determine how a day or a life begins, but we make decisions that determine how both end and where they find us.

- The spiritually-minded person can see God on the darkest night.

- Only the individual can separate himself from God and His power, blessings, and love; the realization of this simple truth may well prove to be one of our greatest blessings.

- Those who take blessings for granted will not take them down the road of life.

- The honest person may not receive all the greatest results but his or her conscience will always be rewarded with another great blessing.

- Some are robbed of a father's love, but if we do not experience and enjoy the heavenly Father's love, it is because we made that choice.

- The head on one's shoulders is much more important than the hat on the head.

- What we want to do and what we do may not always be the same thing; however, doing what we need to do will always produce the best and most rewarding results.

Anger: Sin or Friend?

Do we control anger, or does anger control us? This can be the difference in whether or not this emotion is a sin or if it becomes a friend. It can be a horrendous enemy and a dreadful sin; it can also be an ally and a protective friend.

Few if any have not suffered because of sin. There can even be times when pain produced by anger at one who has done an injustice to another can be in order. Even then it must be kept in proper perspective lest it grow into an enemy.

Care must be exercised always to prevent taking action unbecoming under stress or anger. God knew it could present problems, sin, and pain; at the same time, the fact that sin is part of our emotional being can be useful. Because of the possible misuse of anger, God has given us many examples of anger used wisely and improperly—examples of the results of uncontrolled anger and of proper use of this emotion.

God is perfect. He possesses no unholy emotion. He does have the emotion of anger. He has always controlled and used it properly to benefit humanity. For example, God becomes angry with those who hurt His people. In His wisdom, He knew when it was proper to take action against injustice. He also knew the proper action to follow in every case. We are not always aware of the difference, hence His warnings are provided.

Jeremiah 25:4-7 records an excellent case of God's righteous anger and the proper punishment for improper actions of others. The subjects there refused to listen to God and turned to evil. They even resorted to worshipping false gods. God said this action provoked Him to anger with the works of their hands. He also said that the results would be "to your own hurt." Their deserved punishment by an all wise, righteous God would also bring about good results to others.

This same wise Father knows that there will be good reason for our anger at times. He also advises that we control our anger and not sin: "Be ye angry and sin not: let not the sun go down on your wrath" (Ephesians 4:26-27). Anger does not have to control us.

When controlled wisely it benefits us in two ways. If it is not handled properly, it can result in sin. Sin is always an enemy. If we allow him, Satan will use any good emotions to serve his purpose to our detriment. "If a wise man contendeth with a foolish man, whether he rage or laugh, there is no rest. The bloodthirsty hate the upright, but the just seek his soul. A fool uttereth all his mind, but a wise man keepeth it in till afterward" (Proverbs 29:9-11).

Solomon is saying there are two ways to deal with anger. First of all, we choose our associates carefully to prevent being placed in a bad position. Realize that no matter how good we are, we will meet some people who will dislike us and even determine to harm us. This will provoke anger. Openly expressing this anger in a wild way will make matters worse. It may grow out of control. The foolish person in this position will speak his mind. The wise man will not grow hostile, but will control his temper, think about the proper action, and seek to avoid further controversy. He clearly suggests there are some people we cannot reason with. Self control is always in order. We are not nearly as likely to be sorry and invoke greater pain in such cases as we would if we insisted on allowing anger to control us.

When others witness our self control, they will hopefully emulate it. If we do not, they will suffer pain for following our bad example. That is especially true with parents and children. Should we fail to "nip it in the bud," our anger can produce long-lasting pain. Control may be painful, but the result will not be as bad or last as long.

Uncontrolled physical emotions can result in spiritual harm.

While laboring in the mission field, my wife received a phone call one night from a very irate friend. Lola let her speak her mind then calmly stated the truth about some false information the friend had handled improperly. Then she said, calling the person's name, "I love you." Afterward that person was an even better friend. Such calm action can defuse the other person's anger; the lack of peace can light our own anger fuse.

Anger can excite us towards standing up against an injustice. If we learn to control it, remaining peaceful in the face of another's anger, we can set a good example. I recommend we pray to God for help in properly controlling anger and make it a friend.

❖ ❖ ❖

Misdirected Anger

Our careful examination of anger would not be complete without looking at a very early case of misdirected anger. This is necessary because the sad results of misdirected (as it often is) anger in the beginning of the history of mankind yields the same horrible outcome today.

The first son born on earth first blamed his brother for the consequences of his own uncontrolled anger and then blamed God for the rejection of his sub-par offering (Genesis 4:5-6). When God accepted Abel's sacrifice, the first and best of his bounty offered in faith, and rejected Cain's, which was not his first and best, Cain became angry. God attempted to reason with Cain and told him that his offering would only be accepted if he did what was right; if not sin would be at his door. The results of choosing his own rather than God's required offering was a sin.

Rather than confess, repent, and correct his error, his anger raged out of control. Cain chose to allow his anger to control him rather than taking control of his anger.

The runaway results were the first murder (that of Cain killing his own brother). What began as misdirected anger created revenge, denial, pride, murder, and life-long misery.

His attempt to cover his sin and justify his action caused him to suffer all of his life. Later, God included His warning to future generations of His people. His warning and directive tells us that those who do not obey His word and observe all His commands will endure suffering wherever the disobedient goes, and no matter what he does or may acquire, all of his life (Deuteronomy 28:15-68). This also reveals bitter consequences for the offspring of the offender. No doubt when future generations read this long bit of consequences for disobeying God their thoughts turned to Cain, and they realized that God enforces His will.

Generations later, it is strange that we forget Cain's disobedience and its horrible results; many of us still refuse to make anger serve us as a friend. If we let out our anger on innocent people, we place ourselves in the class of Cain. Any ability or choice our Creator gave us was designed to befriend and bless us—we must choose to control our anger or we will bring pain to ourselves and others.

The Wealthy Suffer Too

It is a very sad fact of life that many are miserable simply because they do not enjoy more material possessions. They often add more pain to their life by holding a grudge and being jealous of those who appear to be rich. Jealousy and grudgery are two major factors in the cause of misery. It is surely regrettable that many suffer because of what we do not have while we fail to enjoy and appreciate what we do possess. The fact is the rich and famous often suffer because of what they have and what they think they need.

Growing up I observed that the children of wealthy people also get measles, mumps, chicken pox, and other childhood diseases just as the poor children do. Also, rich people also get poison ivy, colds, coughs, allergies, heart problems, and lots of other health problems just like those who are not wealthy. In some cases the wealthy children were as unhappy with all their toys as the poor class. In either case most always wanted more and more. What I noticed was the so-called underprivileged child might be as happy rolling an old tire as the rich one was with a new bicycle. Anyone who was able to own a bike always outgrew it before he was old enough to drive a car.

It was also obvious that the rich or poor were not revered more or less for what they had but by how they used what they possessed. Respect was earned by either who helped and respected others along the way. People have always been loved more for what good deeds they left behind rather than how much wealth they left.

Many poor, but grateful, people were less stingy and more generous than those who were considered rich. Both rich and poor people were happier who owned their possessions rather than allowing their possessions to own them.

The conclusion is the wise and happy people are those who are grateful for whatever they own. They share what they possess and find pleasure in doing it. These refuse to add unnecessary pain by being ungrateful and longing for more. Riches are best measured by attitude rather than by dollars!

Turning Pain into Pleasure

Consider these facts that can achieve joy and reduce pain:

Two of the best ways to enjoy what we have been entrusted with and to acquire more are to be grateful for what we possess and to use it properly. To be selfish with what we have is to rob ourselves of both these desirable rewards.

It is not always the most wealthy who give the most and are rewarded the most. It is rather the amount people have and how they use what they have been entrusted with. What one has left is also an important factor.

I have seen some who had the most and lost it become much more miserable than others who owned little to begin with.

The highest improper goals will likely bring one to the most miserable depths. One does well to examine the standard for reaching a goal even more carefully than the goal itself.

I have known blind people who see more real beauty than others with 20/20 vision. I know who is to be pitied the more.

Knowing God well should give us little to be miserable about. To the contrary, those who do not know the Lord find little to be grateful for and happy about.

It is much easier to find happy servants of God than to find happy soldiers fighting against the Lord!

Happy is the one who seeks both happiness and friends in the right places.

It is better to have a hundred true friends than to have a million dollars!

Think on These Things

Here are some more of Jack's proverbs that can prevent and eliminate a world of pain:

- Until we learn that feelings can be deceptive we are more likely to be deceived.

- Two facts about the wisest people: they are always willing to listen to others; they are always ready to learn more.

- Wisdom chooses a road to travel that does not end up at the wrong destination.

- Every choice, no matter how simple, deserves careful consideration and prayer.

- The cheapest purchase is not always a bargain.

- Be aware and assured that a career choice is usually a life choice.

- When one sustains the proper relationship ith God, help is always just a prayer away.

- All of our todays are taking us toward the last tomorrow. A constant awareness of that fact will make both today and tomorrow better.

- It would be better to dwell in a tent with the Lord than in a mansion without Him.

- Even when a bad night embraces us, we do well to use part of it to plan for a better tomorrow.

- If we think life is a game, we must realize it is the most serious game we will ever play, with an outcome that will last for eternity. Let us be sure we play by the Lord's rules!

- A true friend will not always agree with us, but he or she will always have our best interest at heart.

- If a decision is not worth praying about, it is not worth thinking about!

- The size of our heart is always more important than the size of our body!

- True wealth can never be measured by one's bank account.

- We all must decide whether God or Satan rules our life. What a powerful realization to keep in mind. Which one will take us where we want to go?

- Habits are always easy to develop and always difficult to break. That's why we should be extremely careful in developing them.

- A sobering thought—when time has surrendered, how will we have spent it as it existed?

- Holding grudges can strangle the brain's growth. It will also impede our ability to grow socially and spiritually.

- Every question regarding why nature looks and acts as it does can be answered with the same response: God made it that way, or the Fall affected His creation. Any other answer raises many other questions.

- So-called intelligent men have wasted enough resources trying to determine what God has already told us, efforts that could have been used to feed the world's hungry and needy people.

- Wisdom comes as much from the ability to accept facts as it does from research.

- They who work the hardest may not be the richest materially, but they may be the happiest with what they do possess.

- Honesty and integrity will make more friends than dollars and cents!

- Contrary to much public opinion, good morals do not rob people of success and satisfaction.

- Wisdom and hard work are not enemies!

- Work for the night is coming, and those who have labored diligently will enjoy peace and rest rather than remorse and discontent.

- A sign that a boy has really grown up is when he acts like a mature man.

- "Tomorrow is another day" is an old adage, but if that day never comes, where will we live eternally?

- Time alone does not bring wisdom, but rather how we use it determines success or failure!

- If one spends all day sitting on the stool of do nothing, when night comes he still will have accomplished nothing.

- Those who grow weary in well-doing are still better than those who have not spent time in such efforts.

- Solomon asked for wisdom, and God gave it to him; the way we know he was wise is in how he shared this blessing with others.

- Blessed are those who realize that Sonshine is brighter than sunshine.

- There are no sweeter fruits than the fruits of righteousness!

- The Son of God, who has always been, was Co-Creator of the sun that shines in the sky.

- Isn't it strange that some who claim to be the smartest reject the wisdom of our all-wise Creator of all things.

- Only those who accept God can fully enjoy all His blessings.

- Man's own folly is one of his biggest robbers.

- Telling the truth makes the smallest person stand taller.

- The beauty that surrounds us speaks volumes of its Creator.

- Silence may speak louder than the strongest voice. At the same time, God made the voice to speak truth and praise Him.

- If one cannot talk to God and of God, whatever else he says is of little importance.

- Every word we utter today can bless or hurt us tomorrow.

- Speech that is not seasoned with salt is best left out of our diet.

- The smallest flower that blooms may be more beautiful than the biggest. Likewise, the smallest in stature may accomplish greater deeds than the giant.

- How we react to nature often determines how nature reacts to us.

- They who cannot see God in nature are to be pitied for their poor vision.

- What we do with Jesus now determines what Jesus will do with us at the end of the world.

- If we wish to be fully rewarded for our labor, we must have a perfect employer. The Lord is the only one of those, and He always has a good, rewarding job for us. He is the only one who keeps on rewarding when life is over on this earth.

- We are always fortunate to have a good source of water, but an even greater satisfaction comes to those who accept the source of this water to begin with.

- Many of us have learned that physical life is not always fair. Therefore we should be more grateful that we have a Lord who makes all things work out perfectly for those who serve Him.

- Remember that flowers and weeds often grow together, but the wise gardener knows which to cut out and which to nourish. The wise choose the same manner to live all of life.

- To God's people a funeral is not good-bye, but only a space in our togetherness.

One Truth for All — Solution to All Problems

Some time ago I heard a major news commentator make this statement: "One thing I have learned, there is no one truth for all people." The statement is, of course, untrue. Real truth is for all people; lasting truth is for all people.

The fact is that the major reason for division, misunderstanding, bickering, much pain, and suffering is a result of not accepting the proper authority for "the truth."

If one can prove that two and two are not always four, then we can accept the false premise that there is not one truth. It is true that many will not accept some fact of truth because it condemns them or is different from what they always believed. The fact is still that any truth is still true. If we tried to change any truth to agree with everyone who refused to accept it, our entire value system, moral system, legal system, and entire world would be in shambles. If one wishes to have the correct time, he does not set his watch by every person's watch he meets. If one desires the honest truth, he doesn't change his opinion each time someone disagrees. In every case there is a proven standard. If we all accept it, peace and harmony prevail, and much sorrow is eliminated.

Truth is the one thing that's always right. What a powerful, comforting thought that is.

The God who made us is the author of truth. He alone is perfect. He alone can save our souls eternally, and it is He who can provide for comfort and truth in our everyday life. It is as simple as accepting the authority and enjoying a common truth of God. Wouldn't it be sad if someone tried to rob us of that truth? Men have tried it, but God's truth still stands. Many who have fought the hardest to destroy the truth are gone, but truth in every area is still with us. Our loving God gave us a gift we must always refuse to relinquish.

Think It Through — Eliminate Bad Stew

A delicious, healthy stew can be made with the proper amount of several ingredients that complement each other. However, one or a few of the wrong ingredients results in a distasteful, unpleasant, even unhealthy dish.

To prevent such a distaste and disappointment, one must think the recipe through. Life in general is much the same way; if one devotes more serious thoughts to life before he or she acts then life can be more pleasant.

Here are a few simple preventative suggestions:

1) There is a time to sleep and a time to be awake, alert, and active. There is a great danger of misery or failure when we confuse the two or neglect either. In Ecclesiastes 3 wise Solomon presents some interesting, helpful thoughts to guide our use of time. Wise

people accept advice of other wise counselors. Misuse of time is responsible for a huge percent of our suffering and pain. Thus time does not determine friends or foes, but our use of time does.

2) Remember that a small seed or bulb beneath the snow or frozen earth is not necessarily dead, but it may show forth its life and beauty next spring. Likewise, what we fret and worry about or who we may misjudge may, with proper positive thought and care, prove most worthwhile.

3) Blessed are those who realize that real men do cry. It is the one who cannot or will not express emotions properly who shortchanges himself of real manhood. See if you need to re-think your ideas on manly maturity.

4) One of the saddest things I ever saw was a man who claimed to be a real He-Man. He proved himself to be totally helpless when his wife died. He was unable to properly respond to most simple needs without the help of a woman. He could not even prepare some food for himself. As a result, he found himself wasting much time, energy,

and money to simply eat. How much pain he could have prevented by being a well-prepared man.

5) We are made in the image of God, our Creator. When we attempt to change and improve ourselves or others by changing that image, we find ourselves struggling against our greatest Benefactor to our own detriment.

6) The lower we allow ourselves to fall, the further we will need to climb back up and the more difficult it will be to get back to where we need to be. Wise people at least know when to start the climb back up.

7) Whatever goals we attain or failures we endure, we will all end up at the same place at the judgment day: we will be at the feet of God. We can all have the same opportunity of life eternal if we make God a part of all our plans and honor Him now. This may involve a little suffering now compared to the option of immeasurable, eternal suffering later.

8) May we never forget that heaven is a prepared place for a prepared people. With

God's able, ready help are we making that necessary preparation? Isn't it worth even some pain for what we have to gain?

9) Bad things always seem worse at night. With sunrise, many problems diminish to a controllable size.

10) Great servants learned centuries ago that one can feel God's presence without seeing His face. We do not have drawings, photographs, or painted pictures to show us what God actually looks like. It is most difficult to transfer our imagination clearly to others. Great men like Moses could not look upon God's face and live, so it does not make sense that man could view His face today (Exodus 3:20). However, the beauty of God's creation all around us informs us firsthand that God has to be more marvelous and beautiful than the eye has ever beheld.

11) If you find a road that presents no obstacle, it probably doesn't lead to a desirable location. Will the roads we choose result in disappointment or success? Follow directions given by people who have been where you want to go!

12) Refuse to follow a leader who is not absolutely certain where you both need to go. Never lead another down a path that we are not sure, without a doubt, takes us where we both must go. Nor encourage anyone to go down a road that you feel uncomfortable with yourself. We are each responsible before our Lord to make our journey as safe as possible for ourselves eternally and for those who follow us or are influenced by us. A fate far worse than physical death awaits one who leads or directs another to eternal ruin!

13) Even those who have few math skills, but who are grateful, have no difficulty counting their blessings. It may be difficult to count blessings one by one being that there are so many of them. When time is devoted to counting blessings, our time is not focused on our problems. When it seems all is bad, that is a good time to stop and count blessings. Let us be certain that even our darkest moments do not blot the Lord from our spiritual view.

14) Remember one second after today ends tomorrow begins, and with it new blessings and opportunities. The wise person refuses

to allow yesterday's problems to prevent today's blessings. One needs to focus on the new day while learning from the past, all the while planning for the future.

15) Only those who never give up will always climb to the highest realm. The reason some remain at the bottom of the ladder is simply because they refuse to take more steps up. One may always be in the biggest crowd at the bottom, but that doesn't assure his place with the best crowd. The best are still climbing.

God-Given Senses — Friend or Foe?

Our loving Creator gave us five senses; the same gracious Maker placed us in a world that can satisfy all these blessed gifts. We have discussed these senses elsewhere, but I feel constrained to emphasize them again as we near the end of our study together.

Not only did God create a world that meets our needs, but love inspired Him to bless humanity beyond that. Every possible need of mankind was in place before God crowned His creation with His highest achievement; He made a man and a woman to fully enjoy what He had made. He gave us dominion over all other animals (Genesis 1:24). Not only did He supply food that would sustain our body and satisfy our taste, but He made His food supply beautiful for the eye to behold and wonderful for the mouth. He gave us pleasant sounds to satisfy our sense of hearing and textures pleasing to our touch. Flowers and other gifts meet our highest sense of smell. We can see the glorious sky, hear the sweet music of the birds, smell pleasant aromas, and taste an abundance and variety of delicious foods while we sustain our body's needs.

Our God-given minds can attune to all these. We can make wise choices to satisfy these needs, or we can choose to abuse them. Proper, God-directed choices of our blessed senses can benefit us. On the other hand, bad or improper choices produce unpleasant results. The wise, grateful individual is reminded that this same principle applies to all God's blessings. Both present and eternal results are produced by current choices.

May we be reminded also that our precious senses are also designed to serve as marvelous warning systems. We can see the approaching clouds of danger, see lightning, and hear thunder all warning us that impending danger could be coming. We can smell smoke and other offensive odors and remove it or ourselves before more destructive danger comes. We can taste spoiled food or things that would poison, inflict pain, or destroy health and life.

Again, we are reminded that if we choose to properly respond to the warnings of our senses, as unpleasant as they may be, we can avoid more pain.

Eve saw the forbidden fruit that was beautiful. It appealed to her sense of taste, and furthermore, it made her desire knowledge. She ignored God's specific command not to eat this fruit of the tree of knowledge of good and evil. In so doing, she abused her precious senses and took the risk despite the warning, bringing about the first sin and its consequences to all people (Genesis 3). This account alone should inspire us to use our mind to properly control all our senses as our Creator designed them to be used. Like the entire Bible, it is recorded for our benefit.

We must properly use God's blessings if we are to see them as a friend instead of a foe.

An Example of Turning Suffering to Serving

Anna had lived with her beloved husband only seven years when she became a widow. Despite her loss and a broken heart, she remained faithful to the Lord. At eighty-four years of age she was still found in the temple worshiping God.

Anna refused to allow her loneliness to bury with her husband her talent and love for God; rather she maintained a steadfast hope, and what a great reward she received. She seems to have been the first woman to proclaim Jesus as the Messiah (Luke 2:36-38).

Can you imagine how much more painful Anna's life would have been had she allowed her suffering to be fed with loneliness to a greater degree, letting depression overtake her life while sitting alone and losing faith?

I personally know many special widows who have emulated Anna's example and turned sadness into a tool to encourage others, reaping unbelievable rewards. We would all do well to seek God's help and conquer our sadness in faith and service.

Nothing is too Hard for the Lord

When the burdens of life get too heavy and we need relief, we should remember that nothing is too hard for the Lord. Not only will it lighten our load to recall this, but we must also realize that He has the power and will help us.

If we feel that His divine nature cannot understand our woes, let us remember what He sacrificed to help us. He came to earth, giving up His home in heaven, and suffered deep poverty on earth as a physical being. He experienced hunger, thirst, abuse, beatings, denial by those closest to Him, and rejection by some who should have befriended Him. He had to withstand Satan's temptations in order to save our souls. Remember Peter's denial, Judas' betrayal, His trial, the cruelest of all deaths, intense suffering on the cross, and mockery till the very end of His stay on earth.

Why...how did He overcome all this? He had a purpose, a goal from which nothing could deter Him. He felt a need to faithfully do the Father's will. It was not too difficult for Him to fulfill His mission because He felt a real need, a purpose. He knew the value of His purpose, not only for Himself but for all future generations of His creation. Certainly not the least of His purpose in dealing with all that suffering was His love for your soul and mine.

Obviously we need to have valuable goals for our lives. We must also feel a real need to show our gratitude to our Savior for His sacrifice and place a value on our soul, a soul God found so valuable. Always realize that He understands our pain, He loves us, and He provides release and escape, and when this life is over, He is preparing a place for our eternal souls that is completely free from all pain, suffering, loss, and every unpleasant situation. We can have a beautiful, pleasant, durable dwelling place that nothing can hinder or destroy.

We need to have valuable goals for our lives.

Even if we do suffer some, our pain will not compare to our Lord's pain for us. It will surely be worth our fight for faithfulness to receive the eternal reward. This attitude can prevent and allay our pain and lighten our load. Remember, "Oh Lord God, behold, thou has made the heaven and the earth by thy great power and stretched out arm, and there is nothing too hard for thee" (Jeremiah 32:17). Verses 18-19 also provide much comfort.

Chastisement / Discipline

The inspired writer of Hebrews would agree with us that discipline is never pleasant (Hebrews 12:11). As a matter of fact, not only is it unpleasant to the recipient, but it is not pleasant to a loving parent even when justice demands it. In reality it is out of love that we discipline just as love motivates much of our unpleasant choices. Just as responsibility, love, and good inspire us to discipline the objects of our love (our children, for example), so our loving Father finds it necessary to allow it at times. God allows our life choices to reward good and disciplines us for our own good.

The wise Solomon informs us if we love a child, we will chasten that child at times (Proverbs 13:24). Our earlier reference in Hebrews points out that a lack of discipline can disrupt an entire household. At times it is the only source of peace. The home in which parents exercise discipline in love has learned and benefited from that knowledge. The Christian who has learned this in God's family will enjoy and produce peace in the church.

David says, "It is good for me that I have been afflicted; that I might learn thy statutes" (Psalms 119:71). Obviously discipline is a learning tool. We do well to learn and practice the attitude of David and to also accept our heavenly Father's system of discipline as a means of learning and making choices that result in peace and happiness.

When we think of pain and suffering as a friend or foe in relation to discipline, it really depends in large measure if it is self-inflicted pain or if outside force inflicts it. In the case of discipline, our wrongdoing brings on the possible pain in order that we might become better people.

Chastisement, when properly directed by right motives and methods, still causes pain, but God intended that we use discipline to stop or hinder forces, attitudes, or habits that would otherwise inflict more serious pain. When God's intended and prescribed methods are employed, the results are good. Naturally the improper measure and use will result in more severe pain which hinders its purpose. Hopefully our efforts to differentiate between the two will serve to improve the quality of life for all of us.

Also whether or not pain and suffering or discipline serve or hinder is largely dependent on the individual. If we persist in blaming God, our pain can become a bitter, miserable enemy. If, on the other hand, we examine and determine the true cause we decrease the misery and are able to deal with it properly. Our all-powerful God can help us to accept beneficial suffering, such as discipline for our own good, and resolve the cause. Obviously if we cause our own pain we should figure out a way to prevent future pain, such as taking the discipline to heart and amending our ways.

The exercise of forgiveness of one who hurts us in many causes can strengthen us and make friends of those responsible. In such cases we may turn pain into a blessing and become more disciplined in our relationships and emotions.

In his book, *Portrait of God,* Frank Chesser helps us understand much about God's use of chastisement (126). He shows that God does not do what is right in the sense of conforming to a moral standard external to Himself; what God does is right simply because His omniscient way is always right. God's way is good and right because it proceeds from His character. Godly parents punish disobedience by God's standard to ensure good results.

We suffer when we decide our way is better than His.

Though he was a king, David suffered when he substituted his will for God's will. Like men in all ages past, we suffer today when we decide our way is better than His. The consequence of our discipline, if it proceeds from God or a God-approved method, will result to our advantages.

If we, like David, substitute lust for God's law of love then a natural process can produce all sorts of painful results. For example, disregard for God's moral laws produces adultery, fornication, heartbreak, broken families, disease, death, and a host of other unpleasant outcomes.

If there is ever a just cause to place blame on our Lord it is because He designed laws for our good. When we disrespect His authority for our own self interests, methods of discipline are in place to help us learn from our errors so we can have a chance at heaven.

It is also important to make a note about having the quality of self discipline. The lack of self control or self discipline allows fleshly desires, lusts, and such to rule our lives. Pain becomes a natural result. For example, overindulging in any way produces illness and danger. If we are wise we will exercise self discipline when faced with a similar situation and avoid much more pain.

Our all-wise Creator gave us a soul and spirit as well as a body and mind. When we allow our body and mind to rule, not only do soul and spirit suffer, but body and mind as well. When we deny our conscience and suffer its pangs and anguish, we are reminded of the error of wrong choices. Likewise to deny any of God's guidelines produces unnecessary pain. The suffering is not because God caused it. Rather, God knows that the pains of these bad decisions can help us create a stronger self discipline, which will aid us in making fewer bad decisions in the future.

Both God's discipline, though painful at times, and our own self discipline, often painful to build up, help us learn to use our free will appropriately, making wise decisions that draw us closer to Him.

A Common Sense Approach to Prevent or Remove Suffering

Note some tools we all possess which, though very simple, can make a great difference in the amount of pain and suffering we endure.

- We often suffer uselessly because we refuse to change habits we know produce ill results. We must exact every effort to change those habits. For example, if certain foods hurt us, if we eat too quickly and hurt as a result, we must change our eating habits.

- Ego, conceit, and pride all hurt our influence and lose us friends. Why not quit allowing these to reside within us? Develop a true love for good things and good people to prevent being easily provoked and suffering many ill consequences. Love is not easily provoked (I Corinthians 13:5).

- Work on patience! It can be more than a virtue. It can improve our health, our relationships, and more areas of our life.

- Be sure that if we suffer it is for a good cause, and we will find better and quicker relief. Jesus warned of the cost of following Him, but reminded that the end results are glory and joy (I Peter 4:12-13). When we suffer we need a good physician; our Lord is the greatest! We need to live so that He is close and available.

- Remember that we do not always need to express our view. Some things are better left unsaid! A very dear friend expresses it like this: "Taste your words. If they are sweet spit them out. If they are bitter, swallow them" (Bob Faulk). If we want some inspired advice on this subject we should note Proverbs 15:58, "The heart of the righteous studieth to answer, but the mouth of the wicked poureth out evil things." Let us be sure our words fall into the proper categories. We may pay a high price for uncontrolled speech. One moment could take years of our life or cost a lifetime of regret. Think before you speak!

- Holding a grudge is like holding a rattlesnake; we don't know when, but we can be sure that either might strike and harm us at any time.

Stress Can Be a Friend and Ally

Stress is another of our human emotions we all share in common. We can actually devote a part of our concern about stress to allocating it to the role of helper.

Let us begin with ways to lower the destructive stress in our lives. First we do well to examine the cause of any stress. When we learn what causes it we will often be able to steer away from many of those factors or causes. It may simply be a matter of changing a habit or forming a new one. If a problem is related to finances, we look for a better way to manage our money. Any success in this area will produce a satisfactory reward and remove some stress. Other changes easily recognized can be treated in the same way.

Much of our stress is produced by poor management of time. A simple solution may be better organization of time and tasks. The effects of a good priority list will work wonders in our productivity with happy results and less stress. We may even realize we can let go of things that hinder more than help us. Organizing may be as simple as having a designated place to put our keys or other essential items.

Taking care of our bodies will place less stress on them. Eat healthy and eat regularly. Being hungry or having a lack of a schedule produces stress of the wrong kind. Allow some time for entertainment, but refuse to allow too much time to the exclusion of other essentials. Do not eat or drink things known to be stressors. One will be surprised how quickly we adapt to such changes in diet or habits.

We should not worry about things we have no control over. (More on this is covered elsewhere in this book.) Remember exercise is necessary, but over exercising adds to, rather than reduces, stress.

Remember stress is a fact of life. How we control it is determined by the individual. Too much stress feeds another enemy—anxiety.

Stress becomes a friend when it becomes positive stress. Success or promotions can produce stress, but at the same time can evoke concentration and determination to grow and further develop good qualities or better use our talents or abilities by focusing on the rewards of the future. Later the satisfactory relief will come as we produce the positive stress in our lives.

One practice to employ is discipline habits or practices that produce negative stress. This may be as simple as replacing harmful things with helpful qualities.

Concentrate on what we have, not on what we do not possess. We need both willpower and won't power! If we begin by delaying gratification, we will find other outlets more quickly. We must realize the importance of fulfilling our inner potential over our outward, temporary potential or desire.

Every natural ability has a God-given purpose. Proper application of that purpose rewards. Abuse of any ability produces stress, danger, and all manner of suffering and problems.

❖ ❖ ❖

Dealing with the Stress of Life

I asked our son, Deryl Hilliard, to submit a few comments about the pain of stress, a very common source of much of our problems with suffering. He is a marriage and family therapist and the Director of Children's Services and Southwest Regional Psychologist. Below is his contribution.

❖ ❖ ❖

I don't think there is a human being alive who has not experienced stress. In fact, it is estimated that stress plays a part in approximately 75% of visits to physician's offices. This mind-body stress connection indicates how poorly people manage the stressors we all experience.

In the late 1970s and on through the 1980s, several significant theories were developed regarding those personality traits that immunize us against the ill effects of stress. Aaron Antonovsky, an Israeli medical sociologist, developed his Sense of Coherence Theory to describe these personality traits. In his research, he found that individuals who handled stress without ill effects on their health view the world as comprehensible, manageable, and meaningful.

If we view the world as comprehensible, it makes sense to us. Events follow some order and can be explained, and we expect the future to be governed by order and make sense. When it is difficult to make sense of the events in our lives, we need to remember that God is in control and have faith in Him to work things out somewhere in the "big picture." Romans 8:28 says, "And we know that in all things God works for the good of those who love him."

We see the world as manageable when we either have the resources necessary to manage life's problems or know where to find them. We may not believe we can handle our problems alone, but we know where to turn for the help we need. Psalms 55:22 tells us, "Cast your cares on the Lord and he will sustain you." Galatians 6:2 tells us to "carry each other's burdens." So as Christians we can look first to the Lord and then to brothers and sisters in Christ for help when our lives seem out of control.

Meaningfulness is seeing life as worthwhile and life's problems as being worth investing energy in to overcome. One way to find meaning in life is through service to God and service to others. Ecclesiastes 12:13

tells us to "fear God and keep His commandments, for this is the whole duty of man."

If you don't see life as meaningful, manageable, and comprehensible, remember that God is in control, you can call on Him or your Christian family for help when you need it, and you should try to spend some time every day in His service and the service of others around you. In this way you can improve your outlook and also improve your ability to deal with life's stresses.

Our Choice — Good or Bad: Friend or Foe

The beautiful book of Psalms begins with the word "blessed." In Hebrew the meaning is a joyful, contented state. It is so desirable we all want to experience it. The big question is how is this state attained? It is largely a matter of choice. Happy or unhappy depends on the authority or system that governs our life. How can we who were made by God for God's pleasure be happy if we do not serve the purpose for which we were created? Note Philippians 2:13, "For it is God which worketh in you both to will and to do of His good pleasure."

Isn't it strange that we often blame our unhappiness on God? Think of this example: we visit the doctor, and he prescribes medicine or treatment. If we refuse to apply the advice he offers, can we honestly blame the physician if our desired result does not occur? It is likely that when we refuse to follow the instructions, more misery results. In Matthew 5-7 the Great Physician prescribes the means to cope with all the miseries of life, or how to prevent them. If we refuse to apply the advice of the great Sermon on the Mount, what results can we expect? We have been given the blessing of choice! How we use it, what we choose, determines whether or not we make that choice a friend or a foe.

The renowned *National Geographic* ran an article by Francis Collins in February 2007 about this topic. The article does a great job of talking about the discontentment and dissatisfaction that comes from blaming God when our decisions bring us pain. Despite people knowing this truth, many continue to blame our Maker for our suffering. Not only is the accusation unfair, it is most unreasonable.

How shall we use our blessed gift of choice? We determine if it is a friend or enemy!

Pain is Inevitable: Misery is Optional

I noted the above title on the margin of a January issue of the interesting magazine called *Reminisce Extra.*

The happiest people are those who please God. What is best for truly happy people is best for us physically, mentally, spiritually, and emotionally. Genesis 12:1 has the remarkable promise to Abraham: "I will bless them that bless thee." Proverbs 13:13-14 calls attention to a great fact; it reminds us that our attitude toward God's word determines whether we are rewarded or destroyed. To the wise it is the fountain of life that enables us to escape the snares of life. Psalms 1 also shows that happiness or misery, success or failure, depends on whom we associate with. The degree of misery may well depend on how far we go and how closely we associate with the wrong type of people. I Corinthians 15:33 attests to that fact: "Be not deceived: evil communications corrupt good manners." Deuteronomy 30:15-19 reminds that there is a choice that results in life and good as opposed to evil and death.

It is interesting that if we place two bad people in a crowded room they tend to find each other. I have noted that with college students year after year. One not only determines his associates but also how closely he relates to them. Lot pitched his tent toward Sodom, and this was the beginning of his sad downfall. Our entire destiny may well depend on whom we walk with, listen to, and partake with. Usually wrong choices are not immediate; rather, they are a process.

> Usually wrong choices are not immediate; rather, they are a process.

We should determine to learn from our mistakes and not repeat them, which often develops bad habits that become more and more difficult to break. Satan is always busy. He seeks any opportunity to catch us off guard. Once we are caught and realize it, we must determine to keep our guard up in the future. We need to make our choices and not allow the devil to choose for us or influence our decisions.

Just owning a Bible is not enough. We must rejoice in its directions, make proper applications, think about its message, and always take comfort in it. Rejoice in its wisdom. It provides healthy food for body and soul. Matthew 4:3-4 reveals how Jesus successfully resisted the devil's temptations. If we fill our minds with good, there will be little room for bad things.

There is a sense in which we all suffer, but most of the time the misery is still optional.

Find Something Good to Enjoy

A depressed lady said she wanted to get better so she could enjoy her grandchildren. She may have had the order reversed. It seems to me if she would enjoy her grandchildren, she would begin to feel better.

We have had times when our children and grandchildren were coming for a visit, and we felt miserable. When they came, we soon found ourselves feeling much better.

Many of us have experience feeling terrible and yet knowing we needed to visit the hospital or nursing home. We left there feeling much better than when we arrived.

Sometimes we find ourselves feeling so poorly that we don't even want to get out of bed in the morning. Often when we do get up and put our minds to some service or something we enjoy, we end up feeling much better.

At times two family members are not feeling well at all; however, when we decide to help each other we can both end up feeling better.

Occasionally a depressed person feels useless and helpless. If we feel this way, doing something for another person can help us feel vital and valuable again and enjoy a dual surprise: feeling good about helping and enjoying a sense of accomplishment.

We all feel good, or better, when we do good. We enjoy the task and soon realize we are feeling stronger for we are working for the Lord instead of focusing on our misery.

❖ ❖ ❖

Gain from the Pain of Failure

There are times in the lives of most of us that pain from failure and mistakes becomes the only successful teacher. The ill consequences in some cases can make the wise wiser and better.

An unpleasant experience should produce a personal inventory. If when we suffer we ask why and seek a reasonable answer, we often experience a growth process and seek a different channel for our life. In fact, a change in perspective and values may result from lessons learned. Otherwise we multiply our pain by pursuing the same course. Why should anyone repeat a performance that produces unpleasant and detrimental results? If perchance we do, surely we will be even more careful in the choices we make.

If indeed an error in judgment produces a wise examination in future decision, we have grown and become a more mature person.

No child learns to walk without many falls. One who refuses to expend any effort to achieve lest he make a mistake renders any success impossible by making the most unreasonable choice of all. I know of no successful inventor who did not fail a multitude of times. Think what we would have lost if Thomas Edison had become discouraged, finding his mistakes and failures too painful to further his efforts toward his wonderful goal.

No child learns to walk without many falls.

Our thought process is developed by both success and failure, our pain and our joy. Without this team of teachers we would no doubt still live in caves and enjoy none of the blessings God intended.

May we choose to use our mind and current sources of opportunity to wisely examine the choices before us lest we either abuse them to our detriment or fail to use them for the glory of God who gives us all good things.

Hindrance or Life Saver?

A few years ago I became very disturbed at some small incident that delayed me a brief time in traffic. When I did get to move on down the road, I soon approached a terrible automobile accident. It had happened just about the same time that I had been forced to lose a little time. Had it not been for the delay I would have very likely been right where the accident was. It is probable that I would have been involved, perhaps injured or killed.

In more recent years some service men missed a flight home because of some trivial error in their papers. The delay saved their lives as the plane crashed, and all those aboard were killed. Their disgust turned into thankfulness.

How many accounts similar to these could we all tell? On the other hand, how often do we lose our temper and become very disturbed at some small matter that disrupts our plans? Our hindrances, obstacles, and delays may have prevented many bigger problems or even saved our lives at times.

When Joseph was sold into bondage or put into prison or as he endured the series of bad experiences, how must he have felt? When we read this great account in Genesis 37-47 we recognize that everything that happened to him depended directly on the event that preceded it. That includes the good outcome for him, for his people, and for entire nations of people. Joseph later recognized that the hindrances resulted in blessings and lives saved. He told his brothers in Genesis 45:5 not to be grieved or angry with themselves for their ill treatment of him, "for God did send me before you to preserve life."

When we consider Joseph's life, the trials of other Bible characters, and our own past experiences, we should be able to accept the disruptions, disappointments, and delays in our lives with a different attitude. If this does not help, let us remember Paul's statement recorded in Romans 8:28, "all things work together for good to them that love God." The "all things" includes the bad experiences as well as the good.

What Do You Worry About?

Inasmuch as most of us spend a big percent of our precious life worrying, let's take some of our "worry time" and use it to take an inventory of our worries.

A businessman once drew up his own "worry chart" of which he kept a record of his anxieties. He discovered some interesting percentages.

- 40 percent of his worries were over things that were not likely to ever happen.
- 30 percent concerned past decisions that he could do nothing about now.
- 12 percent dealt with other people's criticism of him.
- 10 percent were worries about his health.

As we look back over this list we realize as he did, that only 8 percent of worries were really legitimate. Perhaps our own worry chart would reveal that about the same percent of our worries have any basis at all.

Certainly the things that cause the most anxiety never come to pass. One great philosopher named Michel de Montaigne said, "My life has been full of terrible misfortunes most of which never happened."

Dorothy Dix once said, "When people ask me what has kept me going through the troubles that come to most of us, I always reply: I stood yesterday. I can stand today, and I will not permit myself to think about what might happen tomorrow."

Jesus Christ gave this advice: "Take therefore no thought for the morrow: for the morrow shall take thought for the things of itself. Sufficient unto the day is the evil thereof" (Matthew 6:34).

Few are strong enough to stand when they add past mistakes and future fears to today's tasks. Determine to live today wisely and usefully. It has been suggested that we remember that "today is the first day of the rest of your life."

Paul determined that he would not let the past hinder, that he would set a wise goal for the future and use his present wisely and fully in an attempt to reach that goal (Philippians 3:13-14).

Life is a Grindstone

In my second devotional book I include a devo by the above title. It includes the idea that whether we are ground down or polished depends on what we are made of. Most of our disappointments and sorrows are determined by the same measure as far as results are concerned.

The Chinese write the word "crisis" with two characters: one means danger and the other means opportunity.

During the Depression a man lost his job, his wife, and his home. About the only thing he did not lose was his faith. One day he stopped to watch a craftsman chiseling a stone and asked what the man was doing. The craftsman's answer was, "I am shaping this stone down here to fit up there," pointing to the top of a church building. The unfortunate but wise man realized that all his difficulties down here on earth may have been the means to fit him for a home in God's eternal city.

Those who accept the grinding of pain and disappointment with patience and the help of God make friends of both pleasant and unpleasant situations with a view toward preparation for a far better place than the most beautiful palace down here.

Overcoming Losses of Blessed Senses

In my 2000 devotional, *Beyond Today,* I include an encouraging story about a well-known composer of beautiful music.

Many admire Ludwig Von Beethoven, loving and appreciating his exceptional work. Probably few people know this admired composer was deaf. At twenty-eight years of age, he was told he was going deaf. When he was fifty, he was totally deaf. Even at thirty he was already a famous pianist. It is said that he possessed the ability to provoke in people calm, anger, and other moods through his great music. No attempt succeeded in correcting his impaired hearing. Unable to hear his own music with his ears, Beethoven experienced the music in his mind. His piano sonatas are still regularly performed. There are few people who have not heard of him despite the fact that he died in 1827. He left us a treasure of music that has lived on past his death.

I have a strong idea that had Beethoven blamed God for his loss and given up, we would not still be enjoying his life's work.

Should we have a tendency to blame God for our losses and stop short of our goals, we could benefit by emulating some of the great composer's willpower and determination. His desire, willingness to practice, and sacrifice enabled him to overcome a physical impairment and achieve seemingly impossible success. If we add faith and prayer and allow the Lord to help us rather than cut Him out of our life, our embracing the highest power can overcome obstacles and produce success.

The choice of success or failure is still ours to make: hopefully we will choose not to allow Satan, failed senses, or other distractions to prevent our achieving our own pleasurable success as well as the enjoyment and gratitude of others.

❖ ❖ ❖

I also wrote in *Beyond Today* about another case of a man doing a lot, despite physical limitations, as a past American President. I was just a boy when Franklin D. Roosevelt was President of our great nation. I was a man when I learned he was partially paralyzed. He was smitten with polio in 1921. He began a daily routine of therapy to prevent additional muscle loss and to strengthen those already affected. In 1932, despite a condition that would have prevented many from all activity and service, he was elected President. When the time came for America to fight in WWII, he declared war on our enemies. Famous for fireside chats and powerful speeches that helped keep pride up and morale high, he encouraged folks at home who had loved ones away from home.

His legs wouldn't work, but his mind would. He became the only President to be elected four times. Lola and I have visited the "Little White House" in Georgia where we learned more about our thirty-second President, who spent time there for relaxation and therapy. We saw the car he had adapted to meet his needs—the car many from my generation saw him drive in parades on television.

Many physical impairments and problems can be compensated for by using what we can and do have. The results are not only encouraging to others, but it releases much of the pain and replaces it with deep satisfaction.

❖ ❖ ❖

I would like to share another story of a truly successful impaired person. Despite the fact that he is a quadriplegic, he completed high school, graduated from college with honors, and holds a job in engineering and computer design. Not only is he highly successful in everything he attempts, he is also a great inspiration to others. For example, he regularly sends money for a scholarship fund in honor of another special disabled young man. His gift helps others receive a university education at Freed-Hardeman. This man truly enjoys giving!

Think of the loss to himself and hundreds of others had he felt sorry for himself and done nothing! No doubt he gets more pure enjoyment out of life than many healthy, wealthy individuals. He serves God and others as he looks forward to heaven and looks for ways to help others go there!

❖ ❖ ❖

A very special young man and a very dear young lady met when they were students at Freed-Hardeman University. There was a time when some of their teachers became concerned about them sitting very close in classes. They were also seen talking during class.

All alarms were allayed when it was learned that one of them had a visual impairment, and the other had a hearing impairment. Together, they could do quite well in class by helping each other understand the presentation. Not only did this experience prove amazing to all around them, but as a result they fell in love, married, and, as far as I know, are living happily together today!

We can only guess what would have happened if their physical losses had not brought them together. Could either have done so well in selecting a life-long mate? Could they have married another person who understood their physical impairment so well or who could have helped the other so much?

Instead of letting their impairments ruin their lives, they found the blessing of love through their willingness to help another.

❖ ❖ ❖

In each of these cases, people were failed in some way by their senses or physical bodies. Rather than let that bring them down or make them feel useless, they worked hard and shared the talents they did have, blessing themselves and those whose lives they touched through their gifts and service.

❖ ❖ ❖

Think on These Things

When we reach the end of life's journey do we want to hear the devil say, "I won," or hear Christ say, "Welcome home"? We make that choice now!

The difference in an inch and a mile is not just marks on yardsticks or a space on a map; it also represents experience, effort, true desires, beauty, and satisfaction among other factors. In either case, proper determination can help us reach some goal. What we are seeking determines what we attain.

Selfishness robs; selflessness rewards.

How much does it cost? Usually we think in terms of monetary value. It is safe to include time, friendships, emotion, health, integrity, influence, and a host of other valuable assets.

Very often suffering is caused by placing money at the top of our priority list. Many truly valuable possessions cannot be bought with money.

Some worry about money they do not have. Others worry about money they do have. In either case it's action, not worry, that connects the things we worry about. "Worry no more "deserves the top of our priority list more than money!

Think Again before Giving Up

Discouragement is a terrible and powerful opponent who wins many conflicts. It prevents our attaining many goals and salvaging many relationships. Thinking over alternatives and weighing the value of what we are losing when we give up, just one more time, could determine our success rather than our failure.

For example, when we lose an object we always find it in the last place we looked because of the last effort we made.

Consider this idea: when we give up on some person or relationship we are giving up on ourselves as well as the other party. We are admitting we did not possess the ability, determination, or patience to overcome. Perhaps we are saying, "I didn't love them enough, or I refuse to sacrifice enough to make an important difference." If we give up on a job or project, we admit we were not willing to re-examine the facts or alternatives. Perhaps we were unwilling to seek help or employ other means or resources. We are, in reality, saying this was not as important as we first thought. Each time we give up, we weaken our resistance and admit a weakness that will pursue us to our future detriment. Next time we will be more inclined to reason, "I gave up and survived, so why not do that again?"

When we give up on living a Christian life, we are giving up and expressing a lack of confidence in the Lord who had a great love and trust in us. Our Savior had enough concern for us that He was willing to make the supreme sacrifice for us! He trusted us to be grateful for His intervention in our lives so that we would be grateful and accept His gift. He knew we needed that attitude to remain with Him. We could never sacrifice as much as He did! Why not accept His offer to help us and try again?

If we neglect another person, we are also saying that he is not as valuable as the Lord judges him to be. Or perhaps we refuse to seek His help in our efforts on the person's behalf.

It would be utterly impossible to count or measure the load we accept when we invite the pain of playing host to the opponent "failure." When we give in to failure, we scar our self confidence, have to live with a loss, and weaken our willpower to achieve future desires.

We may find the resources to prevent much pain and sorrow if we not only count the cost of success but also the cost of failure before we give up a goal by quitting one step short of that possession or relationship.

The Art of Happiness

Much sorrow results from an unsuccessful search for happiness. I recently found this material from an unknown author. It could be helpful in changing many unhappy souls' attitudes.

❖ ❖ ❖

You can't pursue happiness and catch it. Happiness comes upon you unawares while you are helping others.

The philosophy of happiness is pointedly expressed in the old Hindu proverb which reads, "Help thy brother's boat across and lo, thine own has reached the shore."

Happiness is like perfume—you can't spray it on others without getting some on yourself.

Happiness does not depend upon a full pocket-book, but upon a mind full of rich thoughts and a heart full of rich emotions.

Happiness does not depend on what happens outside of you but what happens inside of you; it is measured by the spirit in which you meet the problems of life.

Happiness is a state of mind. Lincoln once said, "We are as happy as we make up our minds to be."

Happiness doesn't come from doing what we like to do but from liking what we have to do.

Happiness comes from putting our hearts into our work and doing it with joy and enthusiasm.

Happiness does not come from doing easy work, but it is the after-glow of satisfaction that comes after the achievement of a difficult task that demanded our best.

Happiness grows out of harmonious relationships with others based on attitudes of good will, tolerance, understanding, and love.

Happiness is found in little things: a baby's smile or a letter from a friend.

The master secret of happiness is to live so you can respect yourself and meet the challenge of each new day with the serene faith that "all things work together for good to them that love God," and prove our love to God as we give help and encouragement to our fellowmen.

Continuing Causes for Suffering

It is strange that mankind, with all our progress, cannot learn from the mistakes of the past and prevent and eliminate much of our current misery.

Note the following examples or repeated mistakes and repeated unpleasant results:

- Rejecting the grace of God rather than rejoicing in God's grace;
- Substituting faith in physical or material things for faith in God;
- Trusting the temporary instead of the eternal,
- Replacing love with lust;
- Intruding on the nature of God by tampering with His plan of life and guidelines for worship; and
- Insisting on selfish actions rather than selfless deeds.

The Sinner and the Bird: A True Analogy

One lost in sin may be compared to a bird locked in a building. The bird knows he is in the wrong environment and feels threatened; however, he cannot see a way out. I learned long ago that the best way to get the bird out of his undesirable environment is to turn off all of the artificial lights and open an outside door. When the bird that has become a pest to us and a threat to himself sees the natural light, he will fly to it because he can now see a way of escape.

At times an endangered soul may also experience a dread fear of the wrong world in which he finds himself. Like the bird, that individual may not see a way out. He too needs to see the light only God provides: Christ Jesus is the light of the world. John 1:9 presents Christ as the true light which lights every person who comes into the world.

Unless the bird is freed, he will eventually die. If the sinner remains in the dark dungeon of sin, he, too, will die. Jesus is the way, the truth, and the life (John 14:6). Romans 5:8 explains that while we were yet sinners (in deadly darkness) Christ died for us (provided the necessary spiritual light).

All the painful results of sin can only be removed when one accepts the only remedy provided by the only Savior to remove the dread disease of sin.

Paul tells us the Gospel of Christ is the power of God unto salvation (Romans 1:16). David wrote the encouraging words by inspiration, "Thy word is a lamp unto my feet, and a light unto my path" (Psalms 119:105).

Without the light of the message of God, man is as hopelessly trapped as the frightened, endangered bird. Why must we choose to live another day in dangerous pain when the escape route is well-lighted?

Another Reason Why We Suffer Today

When have you heard a sermon or read an article about hell and its horrors? How many sermons have you heard about heaven?

Usually when we hear the word "hell" today it is used as a curse word rather than a spiritual warning. Less and less often we hear about the glorious reward for godly living and the eternal home of obedient souls!

So long as we are not exposed to the hope of a reward for morally directed lives and the eternal, indescribable torment of immoral, misdirected, ungrateful lives we are unlikely to see the true value of the choices we make. Without this encouragement for good living and the warning about the danger of evil, our world will continue to decline further and further from God. The Lord's people must work harder than the devil's army!

God has always provided two major motives for obedient lives that accept His marvelous plan: these are the joy of heaven and the fear of hell. No doubt both these motives are needed more now than in any period of our lifetime.

Misplaced Blame

Is God to be blamed and rejected because of the injustice in life? Does it not make sense to embrace God, show gratitude for the gift of His Son, and apply Christ's attitude as we deal with life's unfairness?

Would we prefer to emulate Abraham, Moses, Paul, and other great, faithful servants of God or follow Judas?

Jesus never questioned the fairness of God despite the fact that no one ever suffered more tragic, bitter mistreatment than He endured. He was always sad when others hurt. He takes no pleasure in the death of unprepared sinners (Ezekiel 33:11).

We must learn to separate ourselves from the world's ways if we want to live with God. We cannot afford to live like the world by justifying our bad choices and blaming God for the results.

All the pain of Christ and His faithful followers shows what the world is like, but we must remember heaven—which is like a beautiful picture that shows what a loving God is like. Would we throw dirt or paint or otherwise mar a beautiful painting? Wouldn't we be upset at someone who did? If we do not appreciate the priceless gift of heaven then we are not treating its beauty with respect.

If we do not like what we see here, we cannot blame God. We must accept His help to prepare a perfect home at the end of life's journey!

Suppose we read the book of Job (with all of this man's suffering) and became so sad and disappointed with God and Job's misery that we gave up before we read the last chapter. We could never feel good about God or life, but if we complete this awesome story, our faith will be restored as we see God's reward for a faithful life!

From Sharecropper's Daughter to Governor

She grew up as a daughter of hard-working sharecroppers. Later she married and had three sons. She lost her husband while still very young. She did not even have a high school education. Were it not for the background of good parents and proper values, her story would have remained rather bleak.

Our heroine worked two jobs and earned her GED, then worked her way through college. Later she obtained a job in the governor's office. All those around her were impressed with her work ethic and the quality of her work.

In the year 2000 election, she became the governor of Delaware. When asked some of the contributing factors to her success she replied it was lessons from her parents, including working hard and observing the golden rule.

Similar stories could be recounted, all of which make it obvious that hardships which could hinder and create pain can be turned into blessings.

Frank Dunn, a preacher, once said that great minds speak of ideas (ways to make things better). Average minds speak of things (movies, plays, books, places). Little minds speak of people. (Anyone can talk about others.)

If we want to have great minds, we need to look for the good in our hardships, work hard, and help others. In this way we can turn our adversity into something that will help us achieve great things in this life.

Encouraging Quotes from Successful People

Think on these things:

"It is not the critic who counts: not the man who points out how the strong man stumbles or where the doer of deeds could have done better. The credit belongs to the man who is actually in the arena, whose face is marred by dust and sweat and blood, who strives valiantly, who errs and comes up short again and again, because there is no effort without error or shortcoming, but who knows the great enthusiasms, the great devotions, who spends himself for a worthy cause; who, at the best, knows, in the end, the triumph of high achievement, and who, at the worst, if he fails, at least he fails while daring greatly, so that his place shall never be with those cold and timid souls who knew neither victory nor defeat."

Teddy Roosevelt's *Citizenship in a Republic*,
Speech at the Sorbonne, Paris, April 23, 1910

"I do not have more time than other people; I just don't waste it on regrets."

Mrs. Eleanor Roosevelt

❖ ❖ ❖

What Makes People Smart

One's degree of intelligence is determined by several factors, all of which are available to nearly anyone.

To begin with, most of us are given more ability to develop our intelligence than we ever employ.

In the final analysis, people learn by study and experience. We benefit and grow also by examining what others have learned and experienced. The smartest among us are those who make proper applications of what we read, study, and experience.

A small child learns from what he hears, touches, sees, tastes, smells, and feels. When he does or says something that produces pain, he is discouraged from repeating that same practice. As we grow more mature, the intelligent person keeps developing in that same process. The smartest learn from the mistakes of others as well as from personal errors.

The wise individual preserves information for the benefit of others. Likewise, other industrious people apply that information and add it to their intelligence bank and to their lives.

The most intelligent realize that there is available information even from those who do not possess the highest degree of formal education. Sometimes a person's source of information or life experiences will not be available to those who have been blessed by attaining more "book learning." If there are lessons to be learned, we need to use what we have (opportunities and the wisdom of others, for example) to apply that knowledge or make proper use of it no matter the source. Some will even share what they have learned the hard way so that we won't have to travel down that road. We are not truly intelligent if we fail to accept beneficial lessons from unexpected sources.

We are not truly intelligent if we fail to accept beneficial lessons from unexpected sources.

What does all this have to do with pain and suffering? Simply the fact that those who do not use all sources of information are likely to suffer for not using the mind God gave them. The "smart" person becomes smarter and avoids more pitfalls, continuing to grow intellectually. Wise people are also not selfish in sharing their information with others. We often prevent suffering inflicted on others when they benefit from our knowledge or experience. Such is very obvious when experienced parents teach their children well.

All in all, the truly intelligent individual prevents or diminishes suffering by using all available information resources. We need to learn all we can and use all we learn in the best interest of ourselves and others. Such use of our God-given minds can help us practice pain prevention in this life and the next.

Some Simple Pain Prevention Processes

- If we do all we can for a loved one, especially when one is ill and facing death, we will eliminate the terrible pain and weight of guilt when that person is gone.

- Remember those marriage vows to love and honor in health and in sickness.

- Live today so tomorrow can take care of itself. Don't add to tomorrow's burdens by adding troubles to today.

- We can't live in the past, but we can build on past experiences. We can't live tomorrow today, but we can prepare today to make tomorrow better.

- No matter how pleasant today is, remember to be grateful to the Father who is blessing you with lovely memories for the future.

- Why do the street lights go off in the morning? Because a better light takes over. So can it be with death. If we live a good life here, we are assured of a better life when this one ends.

- Make problems work for you. Body and mind grow stronger if used properly. One result is today's problems help prepare us for dealing with tomorrow's problems if we allow them to. Like gold tried by fire, thus removing impurities, our adversities can serve to make us stronger, wiser, and better.

- Remember, if a plan doesn't work, it may be because God has a better plan for us.

- Learn to turn defeat into victory and adversity and loss into gain. For example, a Christian lady had lost her long-time companion. After a reasonable time for grief, she used her experience to help others. She devoted her life to encouraging other widows, doing what no preacher or other who had not known her loss could possibly do.

- We can regain control of our lives by allowing the Lord to take control.

- Be assured: when we climb out of the pit of grief we will be better prepared to climb the mountain of success.

- I have learned that every good or worthwhile experience takes time. The waiting makes what we waited for more valuable and more appreciated. Now when time drags and my goals are not quickly attained, I just realize that the blessing will arrive when the time is right, when I am prepared, and if the goal is good.

- We never realize the importance of the dreams we give up on. If they are really worthwhile, they are worth waiting for. They may be like money in the bank drawing interest.

- It is true that nothing can separate us from the love of God, as Romans 8 promises. Know, however, that we can withdraw from His side. If God is not for us it is because we are not there for God to bless. Read Romans 8:28 often.

- Sometimes we need to allow the voice of a higher calling to drown out the cries of sorrow and desperation.

A Better Life through Health and Wellness

One who reads this book soon reaches the correct conclusion that this author is thoroughly convinced that people can escape much pain and suffering by caring for the whole being. This certainly includes the idea that if the body is to be healthy the mind and spirit must cooperate toward that end. Only when we are aware of that can we prevent many problems and turn other problems into friends that help us.

This is one of the major reasons I deeply appreciate the unique O'More College of Design in Franklin, Tennessee. This college is establishing the "Hilliard Institute for Educational Wellness." Apart from the fact that this program is named in honor of my wife Lola and me, I am also grateful to Christians and friends from several states who have contributed to this Institute. However, the major reason this is appreciated is because it is designed to inform people how education plays a major role in our health. Naturally the results can be a better quality of life and a longer, healthier life.

This program is in its early beginnings, but it is already meeting some of its major goals: currently producing a quarterly academic journal, publishing a book on education due out in early 2008, and developing scholastic workshops for teachers, students, and those interested in lifelong learning. There is no doubt that many who take advantage of this Institute will enjoy good health and life more abundantly.

Success Out of Adversity: The Frank Riley Story

It was our good fortune in our ministry to move to West Kentucky in the early sixties. There we enjoyed a marvelous relationship with some of the best people in the world while working with the Sharpe Church of Christ.

It was there we had an opportunity to work with one of the happiest, truly wealthy men I have ever met. In a very special way, Frank Riley was forced into a position that made him wealthy in a monetary way.

He grew up in a large, poor, hardworking rural family. Because of hard work, good lessons, and great values, he was already rich in the more important ways. Upon finishing high school, he was able to secure a good job working for an electrical contractor. With his background, many would have felt hindered in acquiring a good job. No doubt he felt that way at times, but he never let it hinder him. He had acquired so many compensating qualities because of his background that he was equipped to gain a good position and perform well in whatever endeavor was required of him.

Frank was one of several children in his family who had been brought up right, and all were high achievers. The training he received and the attitude he developed drove him to succeed. Because of those advantages, he was not satisfied with just working and earning a good livelihood. He had chosen a very wonderful mate who indeed was an added asset. Euleene was a great support to him and to all good works she was involved in.

One afternoon while driving home after a hard day's work, he reached a life-changing decision. In his words he said, "I am crazy; I am working myself to death making money for someone else and could be doing that for myself." The very next day this good man started his own business. When I first met him, he was successfully involved in million dollar jobs. His reputation and his success were blessed with continuous progress.

No doubt his blessings came in part because of his greater love for people and right living than for money! I feel certain he gave more money to good causes than many of us will ever earn. Had he not learned to appreciate the really important things that hard work and doing without at times teaches a person, then his life would have been much different. God blessed him for his honest values, practicing the golden rule, and never losing sight of what really is important in life.

Frank and his dear wife reared four good children. About the time the last ones were finishing school, this couple adopted three homeless boys and provided for their needs.

If things in his life had not started and developed exactly as they did, not only would his family have missed some great blessings, but many more of us who knew them would have lost out on many blessings as well.

This tribute to a remarkable man would be incomplete without these final comments. He suffered losses including the loss of a son in a plane crash and person injuries because of accidents. However, I never heard him blame God for anything; rather, he was very often heard expressing thanks to the Father of all gifts. I never knew anyone who enjoyed his blessings as much as Frank Riley! I thank God upon every remembrance of him. I "preached his funeral," but I'll never finish my blessed memories of a man who did such a great job of preaching service and hard work by the way he lived his life.

The Bob Faulk Story

As I write this book, Bob Faulk is eighty-five years old. He lives alone in a nice house in Gulf Shores, Alabama. I know of no better illustration of the purpose of this entire work than this godly man. For some time my wife and I have spent each January in Gulf Shores, and so I have known him for several years. Though the entire experience of our time in Gulf Shores is marvelous, one of the highlights of our visits there is spending time with this most remarkable man.

This war hero was a Ranger in WWII and served in France, England, and other places. The Germans had taken the town of St. Lo, France, and the Rangers were sent to reclaim it. The Germans heard they were coming and gave them a horrible welcome. Bob was shot no less than twenty times. He said there was not a part of his body that was not hit. He could hear the medics talking when they picked him up, but could not respond. He heard one of his deliverers saying, "This soldier is not going to make it." For a long time he could not move, and for three months he was blind. Later he was told that he would never see again; still later he lost the use of his legs and arms.

The more bad news was reported to him, the more determined he was to prove them wrong. In time his sight was restored. When the doctor gave him the news they would have to remove his arms, because they could never be used and would be a detriment to him, his response was, "God gave me these arms; I think I'll keep them." Today, at eighty-five years old, he reads, studies constantly, and does so without the aid of glasses. There are few things he cannot do with his hands. When one of those things challenges him, he uses his great mind to find a solution and get the task done.

One of Bob's most memorable statements to me was, "I'm glad I got shot." He went on to explain, "I was not a Christian, and when I survived my injuries I knew I had to show God my gratitude." He did become a Christian and has lived a model life of service from his twenties, when he began to obey the Lord, until the present.

His wife died when she was only in her forties. He had two sons and never planned to marry again. However, some time later one of his sons introduced him to a young widow who had two daughters and a young son with Down's Syndrome. After ample time to know each other they were married. This opened another door to a work that continues now and still benefits hundreds of challenged young people.

Because of his love for that stepson, he determined to do something for children with Down's Syndrome who were so badly neglected. He and his wife were determined to start a school for people with this special need. They made a visit to their Alabama State Representative and to the governor and persuaded them to help with this important project. They were given consent to proceed. Locating a suitable building, they found some interested teachers and began looking for prospective students. Soon they located a sufficient number to start the school with students of all ages. Little did people know what a service was being rendered to so many families. (The next step was to visit high schools and encourage seniors to prepare to teach special education. Again their efforts were blessed with success!)

"The Bob Faulk Center" started in Butler, Alabama, with twelve to thirteen students. It was difficult at times to convince parents to allow their children to go, but after a while people were convinced it was a good endeavor, and others began to come, the oldest student being fifty eight. Today there are schools all over the great state of Alabama blessing these young people, their parents, and others.

A few years ago our dear benefactor had an opportunity to visit the work he began when the work was sixty years old. A new section had been added to care for bedfast people who had no one to care for them. These mentally challenged people have constant nurse care, and doctors from nearby hospitals visit twice a week.

Still another phase of Bob Faulk's work was training these special people to do many jobs and finding employment for them. He also was instrumental in getting a Boy Scout troop started. He organized teams for baseball, basketball, gym, trampoline, and boxing. They compete in tournaments and Special Olympics at Troy State. This remarkable work is great to behold and even greater when we remember that the man behind it all was a solider, shot and given up to die, discouraged in so many ways, but who allowed God to use him to bless others and therefore received the greatest blessing of all.

Apart from all the unbelievable achievements, this humble, mild, yet heroic character has served as a minister and elder in more than one Church of Christ. He went as a missionary to fields where no one else would go. He still teaches, leads singing, and counsels others at every opportunity.

When I talked with him by phone on July 19, 2007, one of his statements was, "I've been blessed."

When life gets weary and days get dreary, we could do well to go back and read "The Bob Faulk Story."

The motto Bob taught the people with Down's Syndrome when they were hesitant about becoming involved in a new challenge is good for us all. When they said, "I can't," Bob would respond, "What did you say?" They soon learned to respond with, "I'll try."

I would like to take a moment to talk about Bob Faulk's success with his stepson, who had Down's Syndrome. Glen was a small boy when his mother married Bob, and Glen and Bob developed a very special relationship.

Each night when Bob went in to hear Glen's prayers he noticed Glen would end with, "I'm sorry." When asked what he was sorry for, Glen would explain, "I don't know, but I may have hurt someone today, and if I did I'm sorry." What a great lesson for all of us!

Bob had a very wise, kind response for anyone who made fun of Glen's blunders. Note some of these. On one such occasion two college boys and two college girls on spring break saw Glen and began to laugh at him, calling him a freak. In his special kind, wise way, Bob addressed the four: "That's my son; he has Down's Syndrome. He didn't ask to be that way, but God has a use for everyone. Look at your healthy bodies and thank God for that blessing." They all began to cry and ask forgiveness.

At another time a man observed Glen running to catch up with his mother on the beach and made an unkind remark. Bob turned to him and said, "Sir, that's my son; he has Down's Syndrome. He didn't ask to be like that, but God made him, and God loves him too. Do you have a son?" The reply was, "Yes, that's him over there." Again Bob responded in his dear, special way, "Then look at him and thank God he is healthy and has all his faculties." The other father responded by asking forgiveness and saying he was a preacher and should have known better. Bob's precious response was, "No apology is necessary to me—ask God for forgiveness."

A lawyer once said Glen taught him more than he learned from four college degrees. A doctor once said Glen taught him humility and love. Another said Glen taught him he could get more out of people if he was kind and polite. One doctor who had never said "I'm sorry" to anyone apologized to his wife for being unkind when Glen insisted.

It is my humble prayer that when you read a part of Bob and Glen Faulk's story your pain and sorrow will be reduced and a proper attitude toward God and His power to bless us will be put in place.

Indeed God can use a wise, successful man or a child with a handicap to teach and do unlimited good. Let us focus more on the blessings God has provided and less on our own small problems. Doing so will reduce much of our pain and sorrow. Let us think more on serving than being served and see what a difference our positive thinking can make on our life and the lives of others. May God bless you as you try this prescription. May we learn to say, as Bob Faulk says, "I have been blessed!"

Some Concluding Thoughts to Ponder

Some have suffered and continue to suffer because of a weak faith or lack of faith. Thus, they do not believe God can or will take care of them. Sometimes we fail to recognize that His ways are not our ways; His time frame is not our time frame; how He works is not always the way we work. We may not believe His way can always succeed, and we may not have full faith in His promises.

Some have not read God's word and become familiar with what God is like. Also, a lack of knowledge of His word prevents knowing that He never fails to keep a promise.

If we are not in a relationship with God and His people, or if we have not given ourselves an opportunity to know Him, how can we benefit from His fellowship?

Some may not realize that God made us, and He made us in His image. Only when we believe this truth will we recognize the value of being like Him so that we can feel close enough to call Him Father and ask for His help. At times we do not seek His help because we do not know or accept His conditions for a beautiful relationship with our Creator. No wonder some feel all alone; there is possibly no greater reason for pain and suffering. We do not need to choose to be orphans! Our heavenly Father, our Lord Jesus Christ, and the Holy Spirit are the only ones who will always be there, if we allow Them to be.

If we have not patiently and persistently tried God's way, we cannot really know it works!

If we do accept Him, then no matter how good or bad our present is, the best is yet to come.

If we do not accept the divinity of God then we will be governed by materialism: what a disgusting thought!

Man could not have performed the miracle of God, Christ, the Holy Spirit, and the Bible. It is easier to believe the miracle of God created man than to believe it happened the other way around. (Read Isaiah 3:11 and 44:12-17 for further on that matter.) We could not make anything perfect, and God is perfect. We are not everlasting or eternal, except for our God-given soul. Only an eternal being could make and save a soul. If we reject the One who made us, then our future holds no real promise. If we do accept Him, then no matter how good or bad our present is, the best is yet to come.

Only God could provide an eternal home for an eternal soul. God does not change (Malachi 3:6). We can therefore depend on Him. We change constantly; that's about the only consistent part about us! Let us make sure our changes do not pull us away from our Father and our chance at heaven.

The true and living God can meet our every need now and eternally. When we accept that truth, we know that God is able to see us through every conflict and make all things work for our good (Romans 8:28). Our confidence in this fact blesses us in two ways: it can help us look for the value to our agonies, and it removes and reduces much of our pain and suffering! Accepting and obeying God reduces sorrow and multiplies joy.

About The Author

Jack Hilliard, a native of West Tennessee, received his Bachelor's degree from Freed-Hardeman University and his Master's degree in Counseling and Guidance from the University of Memphis.

He and his family have lived in three states, Bermuda, the Appalachian Mountains, and, for the last thirty-two years, Henderson, Tennessee. His wife of fifty-six years is Lola Carter Hilliard. The couple has three children, four grandchildren, and three grandchildren-in-law. Jack has preached on the radio for fourteen years, written regular newspaper articles for over seventeen years, and made several appearances on live television programs throughout his life. He has counseled on marriage, finances, and health as well as mental, physical, and spiritual problems.

Having served in public relations for an insurance company and two colleges, Hilliard also has sales experience and has owned two businesses. Jack served as president and vice president of civic clubs, president of three PTA organizations, board member of three children's homes, and chairman of the Jellico Area Health Council. He has traveled from coast to coast and visited eleven countries. One such trip to the Bible Lands gave Jack the opportunity to make slides and share lectures on his experience.

Jack worked for eighteen years with Freed-Hardeman University: in admissions for five years, as Director of Placement for ten years, and as Director of Church Relations. His wife, Lola, worked many of those years by his side, and the couple retired in 1994. Since retirement he has been busy with mission work, teaching, traveling, and writing. This is his seventh book.

Printed in the United States
204132BV00003B/1-87/P

9 780980 028508